Insatiable Curiosity

Leonardo: The Artist, The Genius, The Legend

JUSTIN SMITH

LIGHTNING
GUIDES

Contents

VISTA

IN FOCUS

Executive Editor
Jenny Croghan

Commissioning Editor
Alex Stavrakas

Managing Editor
Elizabeth Castoria

Development Editor
Jeremy Dillahunt

Creative Director
Frances Baca

Art Director
Felicia Reyes

Photo Editor
Caroline Lee

Production Designer
Evelyn Whitburn

Publisher
Benjamin Wayne

info@lightningguides.com

ON THE COVER
In his piece, *Jokowned*, artist Clément Chapon captures the puckish spirit of the *Mona Lisa*. Mr. Chapon imagines a modern-day incarnation of the masterpiece's subject would be a rebel, and highlights that notion with this anachronistic work. www.cl3m.com

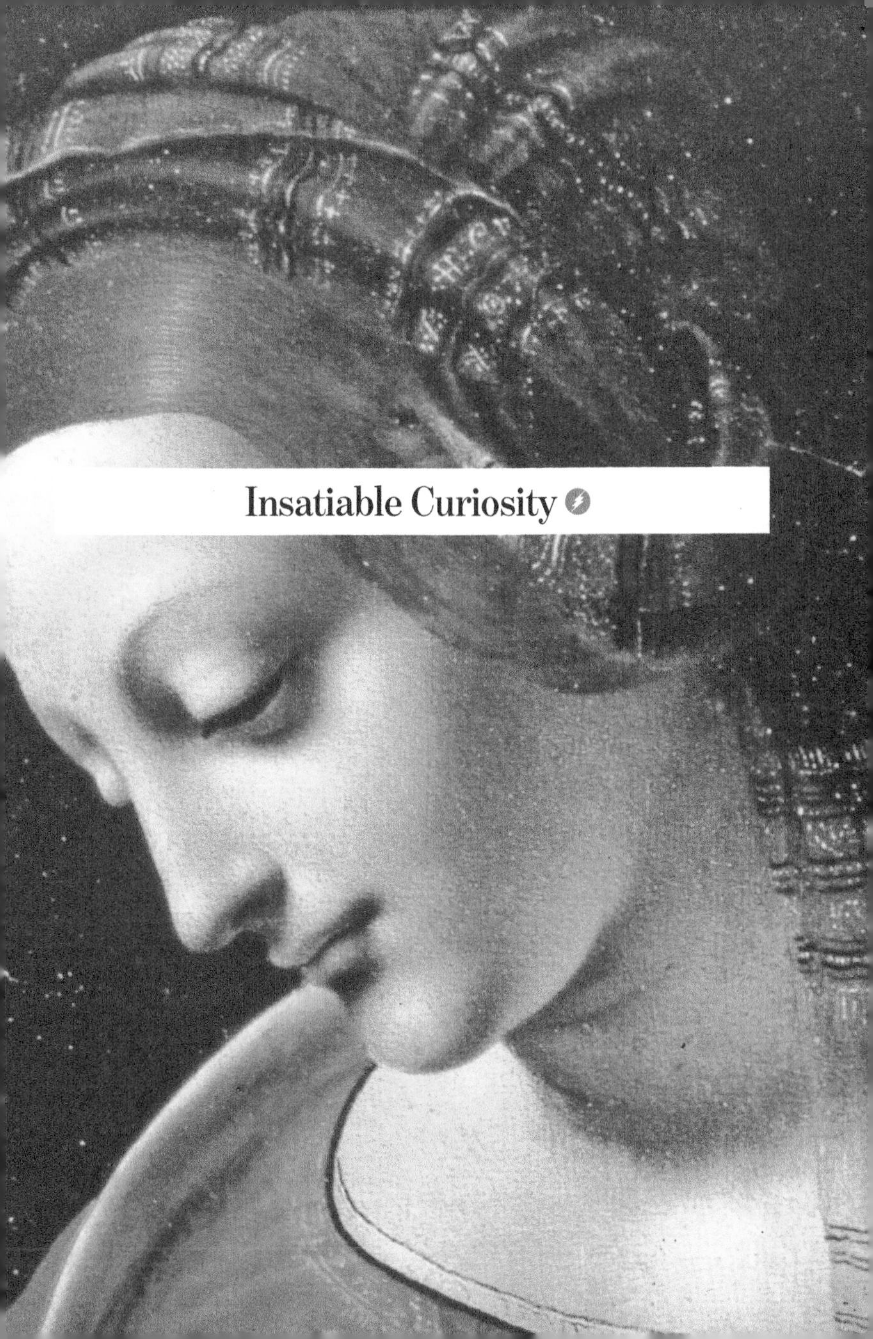
Insatiable Curiosity

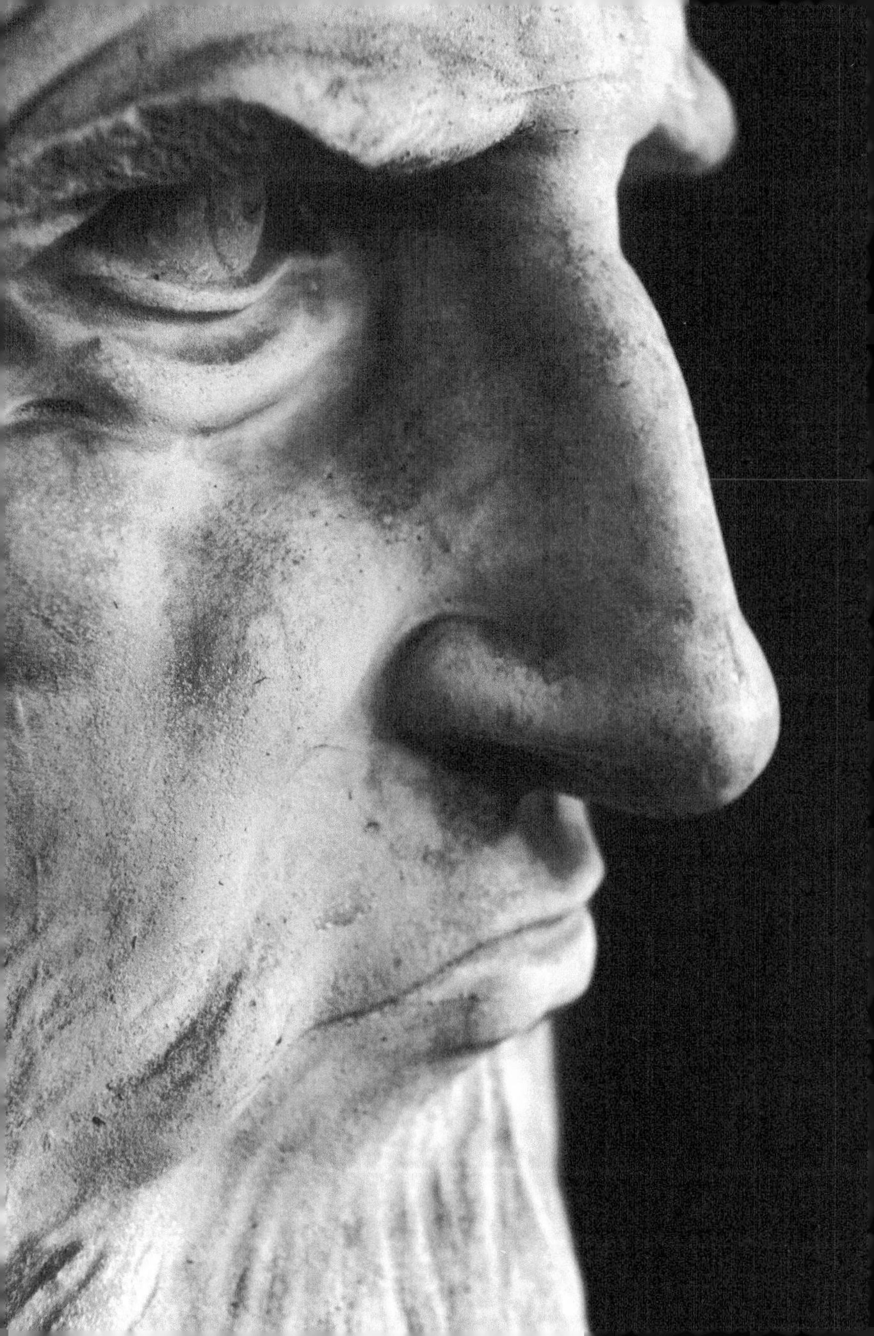

PERSPECTIVE

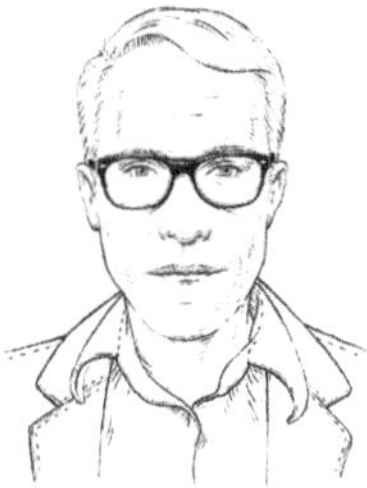

AUTHOR

JUSTIN SMITH

Justin Smith is professor of history and philosophy of science at the University of Paris 7—Denis Diderot. He is the author, most recently, of *The Philosopher: A History in Six Types*, and writes frequently for the *New York Times*, *Harper's*, *Cabinet*, and other publications.

VIEWPOINT

Painting No. 779

A timeless mystique draws today's pilgrims

» **I'm here again**, at the Louvre, with its mega-mall structure, its metal detectors, its hordes of tourists. What are they all here to see? What is the force that pushes them along?

I. M. Pei's pyramids mark out the museum's subterranean entrance, and stand out sharply in the middle of the court against the august wings of the Old Louvre palace surrounding it.

The ebullient crowds with their selfie sticks, the desperate immigrant vendors with their bottled water and Eiffel Tower trinkets. An Italian man is holding a stick with a red piece of fabric tied at one end, moving with purpose, and the group of retired tourists behind him are following

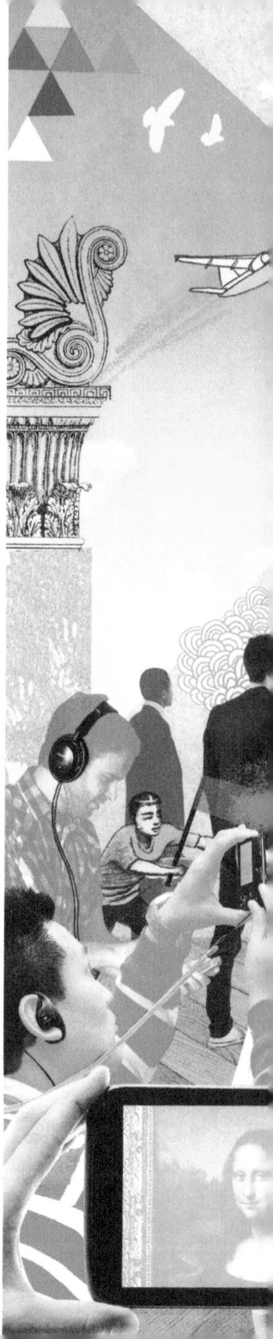

TONWEN JONES / COLAGENE.COM © 2015

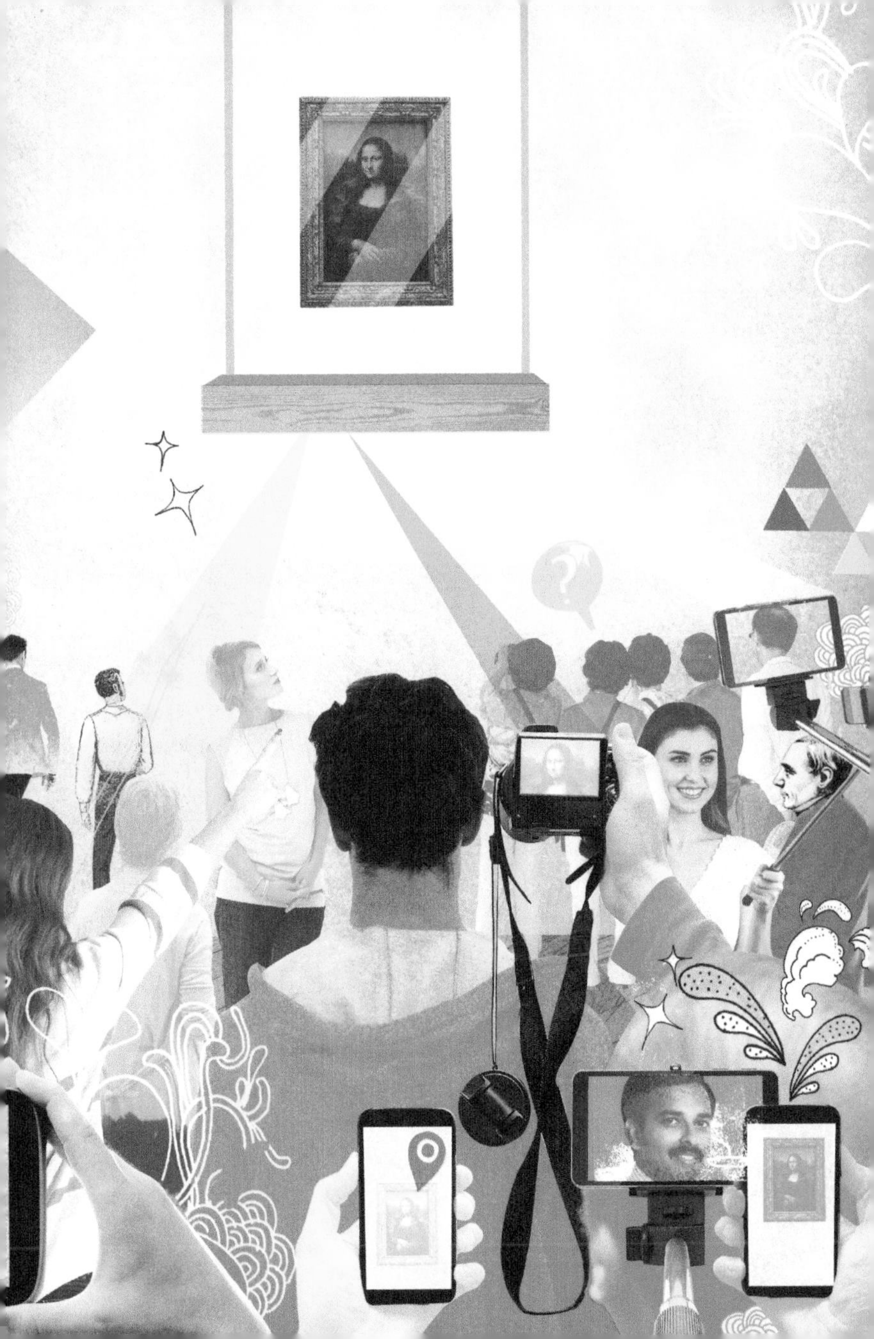

docilely, every gesture an expression of their submission to him, their trust, their temporary inability to navigate the basic features of their physical environment on their own. The tourists are weighed down by cameras and hip packs, they are wearing comfort shoes and visors, and their heads swivel as if to take it in all at once. But, despite the fact that the Louvre's collection numbers over 380,000 objects, they are moving as if there could be no question of priorities, straight toward a great banner over the entry to the Denon Wing which indicates the presence within of the smiling Lisa Gherardini, more commonly known as *Mona Lisa*.

Neither the *Mona Lisa* nor its creator are in any meaningful sense Italian; they belong to the world.

All nations of the world crash together in their mutual purpose: Italian, Chinese, and American tourists commingle as their guides shout out in their native tongues the history they are walking under, the majesty of the institution, and the glory of what they are about to see. Although they could, those who have come from Milan are not approaching the *Mona Lisa,* out of regional pride and ownership. They might know that the painting ended up in France as a result of King Francis I's patronage of Leonardo da Vinci, that the painter himself had brought the portrait with him to France in 1515 or 1516, and that the king had made it the nucleus of what would later become the greatest collection of art in the world. But neither the *Mona Lisa* nor its creator are in any meaningful sense Italian; they belong to the world.

"Oh my God, there it is!" shouts a woman from the American group. People point, squeal, and jump in order to see over each other's heads. "It" is a diminutive portrait, just 20 by 30 inches, of a smiling woman, hung behind what looks like bulletproof glass but is in fact a protection from camera flashes, which are flickering as they would for a celebrity. Some dissidents grumble to the effect that the painting is too small, that it is obscured by its glass protection, that there are too many people in front of it—as if they themselves were not among these people. As if it were possible to visit the *Mona Lisa* without becoming part of the throng.

In some parts of the world today, crowds of people move together, as a mass, to catch a glimpse of the relics of saints or of some miracle-working idol. In Europe, these pilgrimages have decreased over the past century or two to a mere trickle. Tourism, meanwhile, is booming, with France and Italy, Leonardo's two homes, drawing a combined total of more than 100 million visitors per year. People fly from across the globe to check off recommended sites in some mental checklist, to take pictures in front of these sites, to reassure themselves they've seen one more of the things one must see before dying. There is no longer any conscious theology or adoration of sacred objects behind this, but the bare form of the old religious journey remains.

This is a secular pilgrimage, and every pilgrim experiences his or her own illumination upon seeing *Mona Lisa*'s smile. The crowds that come to see Leonardo da Vinci's most charged and powerful relic may be mostly unreflective about their reasons for being here. But the reasons are deep, and to draw them out is to learn a great deal about the modern world.

A VISUAL LEGACY, STROKE BY STROKE

PAINTINGS ATTRIBUTED
TO LEONARDO DA VINCI

Madonna Litta 1490, Hermitage

The Madonna of the Yarnwinder 1501, Scottish National Gallery

Madonna of the Carnation 1472–78, Alte Pinakothek

Benois Madonna 1478–81, Hermitage

Virgin of the Rocks *(later version)* 1491–1508, National Gallery

Virgin of the Rocks *(early version)* 1483–86, Louvre

Portrait of Isabella d'Este 1499–1500, Louvre

The Virgin and Child with St. Anne 1510–13, Louvre

Mona Lisa 1503–07, Louvre

St. John the Baptist 1513–16, Louvre

Ginevra de' Benci 1474–78 National Gallery of Art

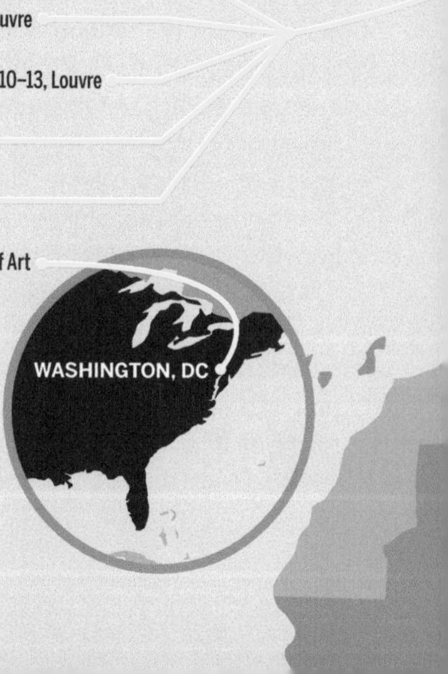

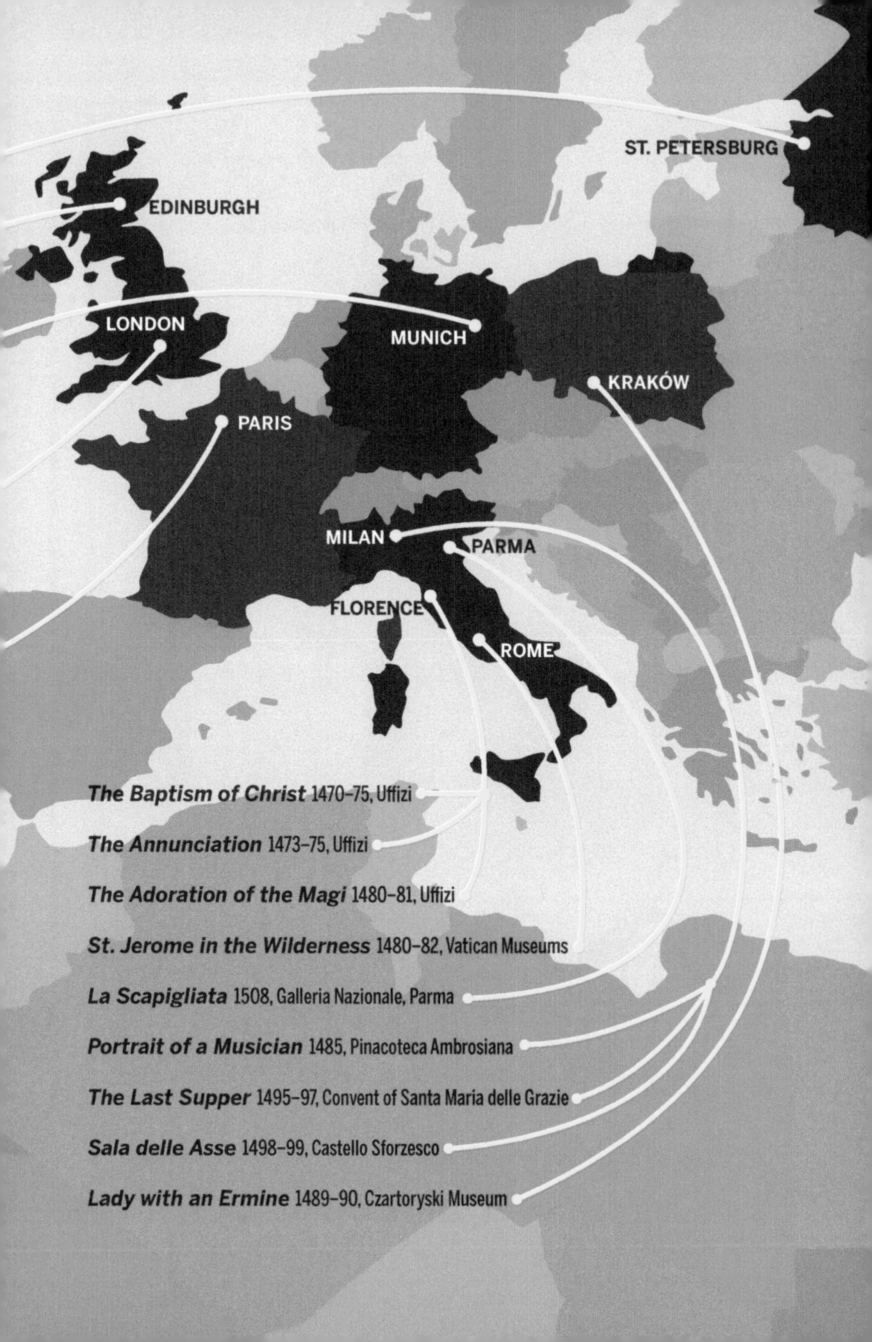
ST. PETERSBURG
EDINBURGH
LONDON
MUNICH
KRAKÓW
PARIS
MILAN
PARMA
FLORENCE
ROME
The Baptism of Christ 1470–75, Uffizi
The Annunciation 1473–75, Uffizi
The Adoration of the Magi 1480–81, Uffizi
St. Jerome in the Wilderness 1480–82, Vatican Museums
La Scapigliata 1508, Galleria Nazionale, Parma
Portrait of a Musician 1485, Pinacoteca Ambrosiana
The Last Supper 1495–97, Convent of Santa Maria delle Grazie
Sala delle Asse 1498–99, Castello Sforzesco
Lady with an Ermine 1489–90, Czartoryski Museum

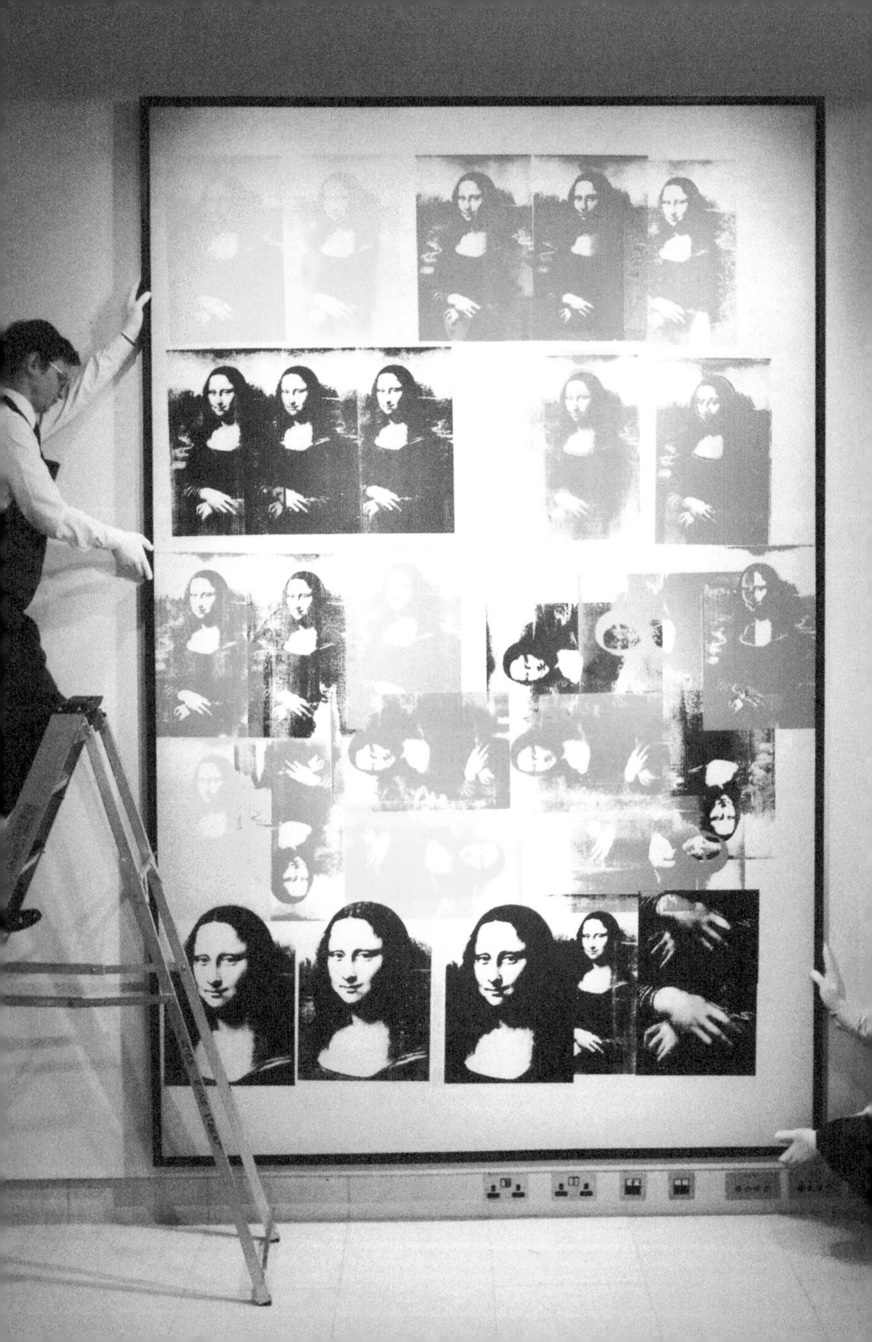

Pop Before There Was Pop

Leonardo transcends the status of a historic master

Leonardo is a superstar. If his contemporaries, Botticelli and Titian, are comparable to indie-rockers with idiosyncratic aesthetic sensibilities and small, loyal followings, Leonardo is the one who fills stadiums, who breaks out and enjoys global recognition. Leonardo da Vinci should be referred to simply as Leonardo, since historians have yet to identify his last name; da Vinci simply means "of the town of Vinci." This places him in the same historical class as Caesar, Alexander, or Aristotle. And, like his counterparts', Leonardo's work belongs to the world.

What explains this universality? It is perhaps significant that many people falsely believe NASA selected Leonardo's drawing *The Vitruvian Man* to adorn the outside of its *Pioneer* spacecraft as it careened out of our solar system. In fact, the image on the *Pioneer* plaque was of a generic man and

La Gioconda*'s pop art incarnation, seen in Andy Warhol's 1963* Colored Mona Lisa, *fetched over $56 million in 2015.*

woman, iconographically anchored in the 1970s. Leonardo's man, by contrast, is the universal man, standing in for all men. Unlike the *Pioneer* plaque, his man is unaccompanied by a woman, and presumably he is held by the artist to contain the idea of woman within him as a potentiality. He is, or would have been, the universal man, hurtling out into the universe.

It is not coincidental that we speak of a man as "universal," invoking the adjectival form of "universe," and thus of a near-synonym of "world" or "cosmos." There is perhaps no motif more central to Renaissance thought than the idea that an individual human being is a microcosm of the world as a whole: both physically, in that the human body is somehow, in its proportions and organic interconnection, an instantiation of the same principles around which the celestial and terrestrial spheres are organized; and abstractly, in that the individual human mind somehow contains knowledge of all the truths of nature and the divine. A German synonym for "Renaissance man" is *Universalgelehrter*: the person who is universally learned. What this refers

Did You Know

Before making it big with his 2003 book capitalizing on the fame and accomplishment of Leonardo—*The Da Vinci Code*, which went on to sell 80 million copies—Dan Brown released a children's album of synthesizer music with a song about joyful amphibians. He also co-wrote a book with his wife titled *187 Men to Avoid: A Survival Guide for the Romantically Frustrated Woman*, under the low-security pseudonym Danielle Brown.

to, practically, is a person who takes an interest in all manner of things, just as Leonardo inquired into botany, paleontology, hydraulics, aeronautics, and so on. It also suggests something more profound, and perhaps a mystical ideal that has been forgotten in the intervening centuries: that the truly learned man is in effect channeling the whole universe through his mind and hands—he is a sort of mirror of the universe, or even identical to it.

When we call Leonardo a "universally learned" man, then, we do not just mean that he was interested in many things. What we mean is that his absorption of as much of the world around him as he could take in gave him a universal quality, and enabled him to stand as a symbol of humanity's highest aspirations and accomplishments. This is the story behind Leonardo's enduring popularity and, perhaps, explains his transcendent fame.

Yet there is a certain darkness mixed in with the great light that Leonardo sought to shine on the world and our place in it, a chiaroscuro quality. In the popular imagination there are hints of evil lurking in the life, work, and legacy of the great painter: conspiracies of renegade religious orders, or of the Freemasons, or of the devil himself. Think of the popularity

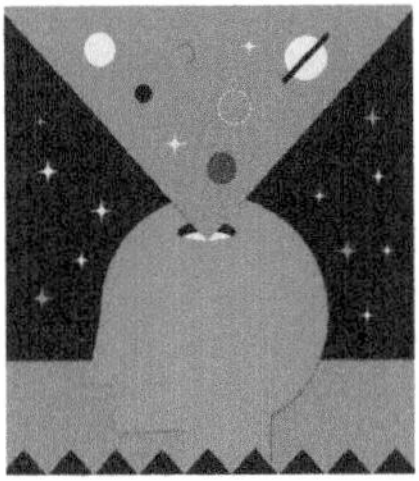

In the Renaissance, perhaps no idea was more deeply entrenched than that of the human being as a microcosmos of the entire world. It was believed that the general features of the cosmos as a whole had to be somehow epitomized in human beings themselves. For example, a common line of reasoning was to infer the number of planets—seven, it was thought—from the fact that there are seven openings in the head.

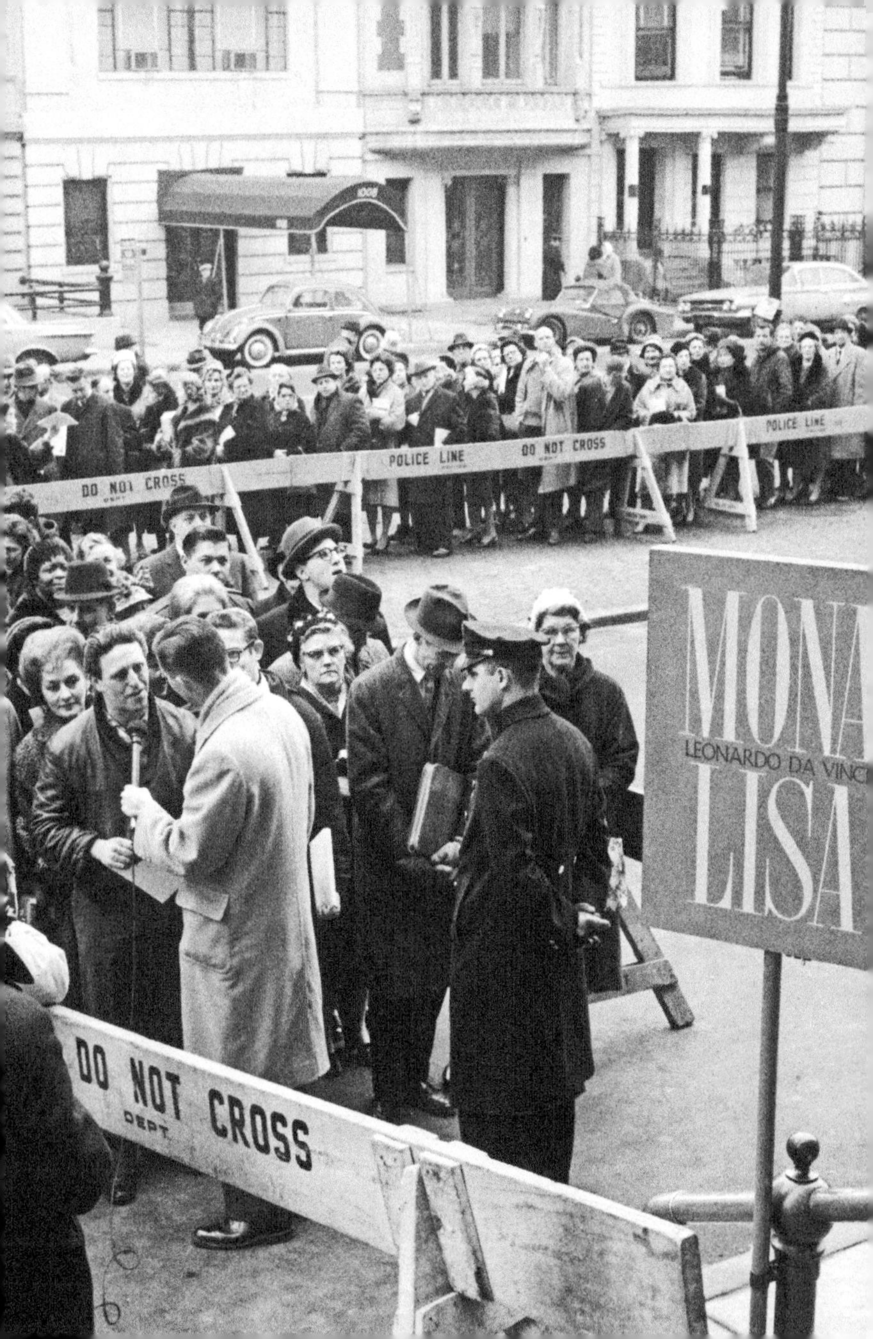
DO NOT CROSS
POLICE LINE
DO NOT CROSS
POLICE LINE
MONA
LEONARDO DA VINCI
LISA
DO NOT CROSS

of Dan Brown, who made explicit what has been felt all along: that where there is a master such as Leonardo, there must be a "code," something hidden that explains the great universal light. Brown is now among the best-selling authors in history, but his own superstar status is derivative of Leonardo's. The reason why his story sold so well is, in part, because it resonates with the Catholic church's longstanding beliefs and teachings that curiosity and intellectual exploration can usurp God's place in the universe. Leonardo da Vinci never sought to do that, but he certainly stands for both sides of that coin: humanity's nearly unlimited potential can lead to the destruction of all it holds dear.

A Dangerous Pursuit

Throughout the Christian era, and increasingly from the dawn of the Renaissance, there has been a consistent concern that probing into the hidden workings of nature is a satanic endeavor, for it is to look where God has not invited us to look. The invention of complex machines, the cutting open of bodies, the draining of swamps: all of these things are against nature to the extent that they are an intrusion into, or a reversal of, what would happen if things were left to their ordinary course.

Such unnatural undertakings were commonly called "philosophy" in Leonardo's time. To "philosophize" was to look into the workings of the heavens above and the earth below. This is a sense of the term that extends all the way back to the trial of Socrates in Athens, and it is perhaps the primary sense

---

Over a million people went to see the Mona Lisa *in 1963 during her three-and-a-half-week stay at the Metropolitan Museum of Art in New York City.*

of the term in the Italian Renaissance. Thus, while Leonardo wrote very little, and neither speculated in treatises on the nature of truth, nor attempted to prove the existence of God, he was, by Renaissance standards, a consummate philosopher and a provocateur. Giorgio Vasari, the author of the important work *Lives of the Most Eminent Painters, Sculptors, and Architects*, describes Leonardo's "philosophical studies" during his time in Rome in the service of Pope Leo X, in 1513, as follows:

> *[F]orming a paste of a certain kind of wax, as [Leonardo] walked he shaped animals very thin and full of wind, and, by blowing into them, made them fly through the air, but when the wind ceased they fell to the ground. On the back of a most bizarre lizard, found by the vine-dresser of the Belvedere, he fixed, with a mixture of quicksilver, wings composed of scales stripped from other lizards, which, as it walked, quivered with the motion; and, having given it eyes, horns, and beard, taming it, and keeping it in a box, he made all his friends, to whom he showed it, fly for fear.*

The following year, Leonardo would be denounced to the same pope for his anatomical and scientific inquiries. Creating new knowledge was—and is—a delicate balance: the examination of the order of nature can heighten the veneration of God as nature's creator and architect but, from the point of view of the church, probing too far into the order of nature can also cause a person to feel prideful in his knowledge, and to seek to replace God with a new power over nature that this new knowledge provides him.

Leonardo probed very deeply. We know this mostly from his drawings and his notebooks. He wanted to figure out how birds fly, and to create wing suits for human beings based on the principles of avian aeromechanics. He sought to create new weapons for battle, including a giant crossbow. He imagined helicopters and crank-driven automobiles. He depicted men and women in the middle of sexual intercourse, hemisected down the center of their bodies in the middle of the act, so that the inner workings of their organs might be better observed. He drew fetuses inside the womb, and speculated on the origins of fossils.

If anyone was ever guilty, then, of the crime of "philosophizing" it was Leonardo. He surely did not think of himself as going against nature but, again, the sort of curiosity Leonardo embodies has always carried with it the threat of trespass.

An Unknown Threat

There is still another sense, perhaps not entirely unrelated, in which Leonardo's life and passions have been thought to be *contra naturam*, or against the natural order of things: he was, at the age of 24, accused of sodomy, a scandal that seems to have had considerable consequences on his life. He appears to have subsequently had long-term sexual or romantic relationships with two other men—to have been, in short, "gay." This is a historically conditioned category, of course, and whatever his orientation, the cultural context in which he and his contemporaries understood it was surely not ours. But this much is clear: his loves were forbidden and harshly judged (though not, it is important to emphasize, by everyone), and this defining characteristic of his erotic life, we may confidently speculate, gave a particular charge to all of

The Nude Gioconda *is thought to be a copy of a lost original, painted not by Leonardo but by a purported lover, Salaì, whose face strongly resembled Gioconda's.*

his life's projects. The art, the invention, the probing, all of them are, we may say, erotic. Not because a gay man is more sexual by nature, but because a man of the Renaissance who desires other men, and who understands desire and creation in basically platonic terms (love as a spiritual, intellectual, or physical pursuit is essentially non-erotic and non-physical, after all) cannot help but see all manifestations of desire—creation, knowledge, love—as expressions of one and the same orientation.

For centuries, the preferred historiographical line was that Leonardo, apart from his youthful dalliance, was too engrossed in his projects to pay attention to the lust of the body. Many of his drawings tell a different story, not least the pornographic sketches focused on his pupil, servant, and lover, Gian Giacomo Caprotti da Oreno, who was called by the affectionate name Salaì ("devil," "dirty one," "scoundrel"). The saintly portrayal of Leonardo is the predominant one transmitted through most respected biographies until the late 20th century. But several clues suggest that his full complexity as a living, desiring human being was never entirely forgotten or, for that matter, excused.

It is in part this lived experience—as a man, as an illegitimate child, as a protégé of popes and kings—that would place Leonardo as the universal, quintessentially modern man: the man who retains, 500 years after his death, the iconic status of a star.

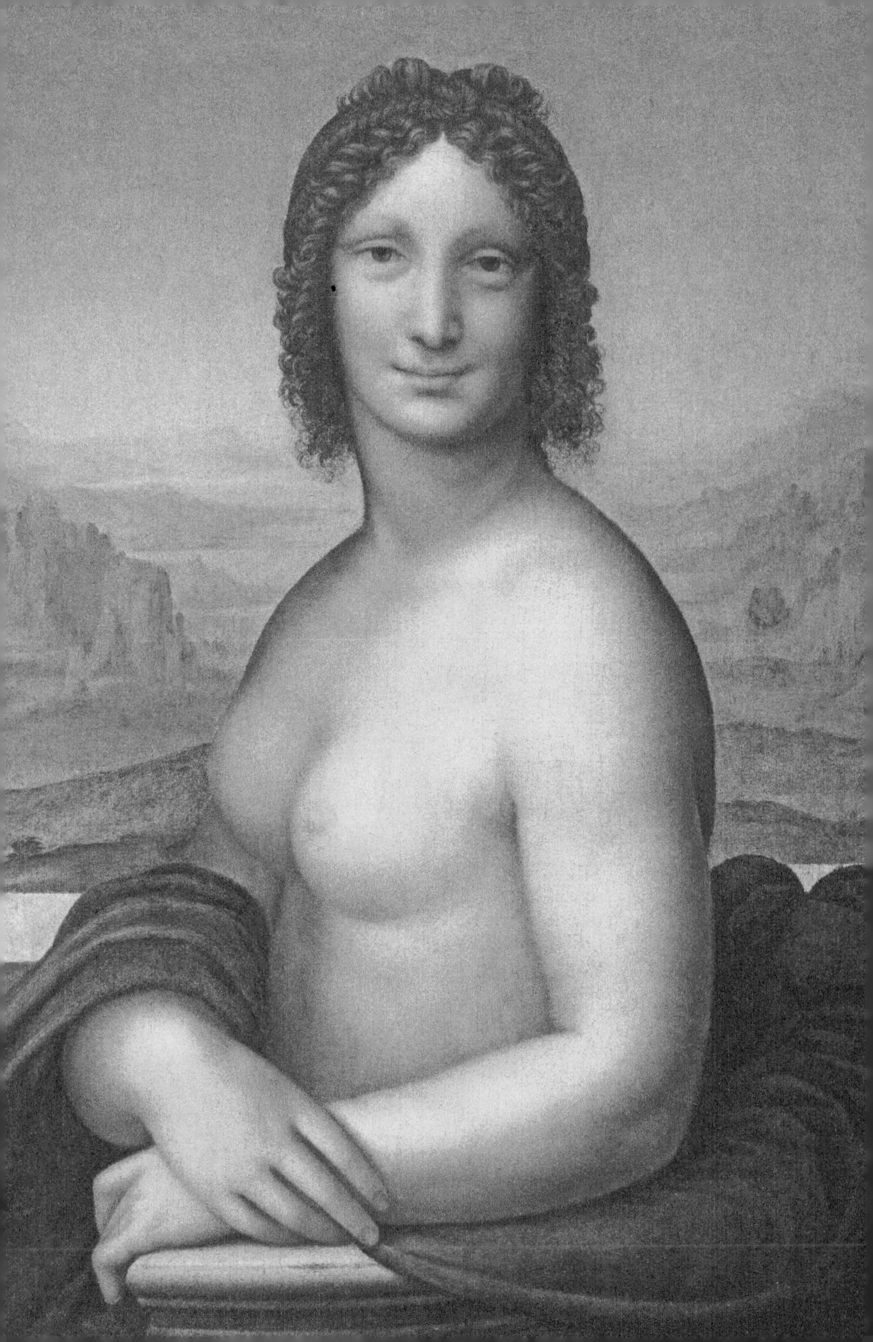

In His Time

ALCHEMY, THE PRINTING PRESS, AND THE ARABIC INFLUENCE

Renaissance means "rebirth." But what exactly was reborn in the period in which Leonardo lived? Ordinarily we understand this term to signify the emergence out of the medieval period, or Dark Ages, which extended from the end of the Roman Empire to the 14th century. The appreciation of learning, of beauty, of discovery, and of invention that was supposed to have been cultivated in ancient Greece, and derivatively in ancient Rome, was reborn in Europe—first in Italy, and subsequently in Northern Europe. In truth, this process had much to do with cross-Mediterranean influences; in particular, with the transmission and translation of Arabic science and philosophy, traditions which had much more effectively preserved the knowledge of the pre-Christian classical world than those in Europe had. This debt usually went unacknowledged, yet much of Leonardo's learning—in alchemy, for example, or in hydraulics, or ornithology—builds on centuries-old precedents filtering in from the Islamic world.

From East Asia, meanwhile, the technology of printing made its appearance in Europe for the first time at the end of the 15th century with the Gutenberg printing press. In 1492, Jews and Muslims were forced to either convert or flee the Iberian peninsula, and Columbus arrived in the Caribbean and began a

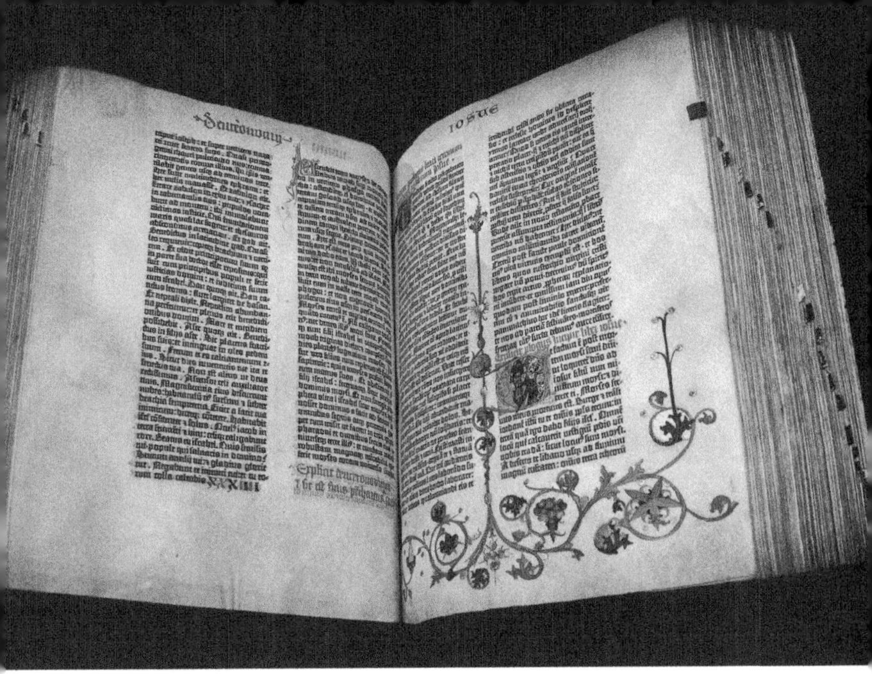

Leonardo's worldview was shaped by the technological leaps of his time, such as the first printing of the Gutenberg Bible circa 1453 in Mainz, Germany.

new chapter of European history by effectively tying the fate of the old world to the newly encountered one across the ocean. Some have said that Europe as we know it was born at the moment it began to see itself in the mirror of America. There was a massive historical transformation underway, of which Leonardo's life is, in important respects, a reflection.

Leonardo himself did not reflect on the significance of the discovery of America, or the development of the printing press, or any number of other important developments of the late Renaissance. But the indirect influence of these global transformations unmistakably informed his work, and indeed made it possible.

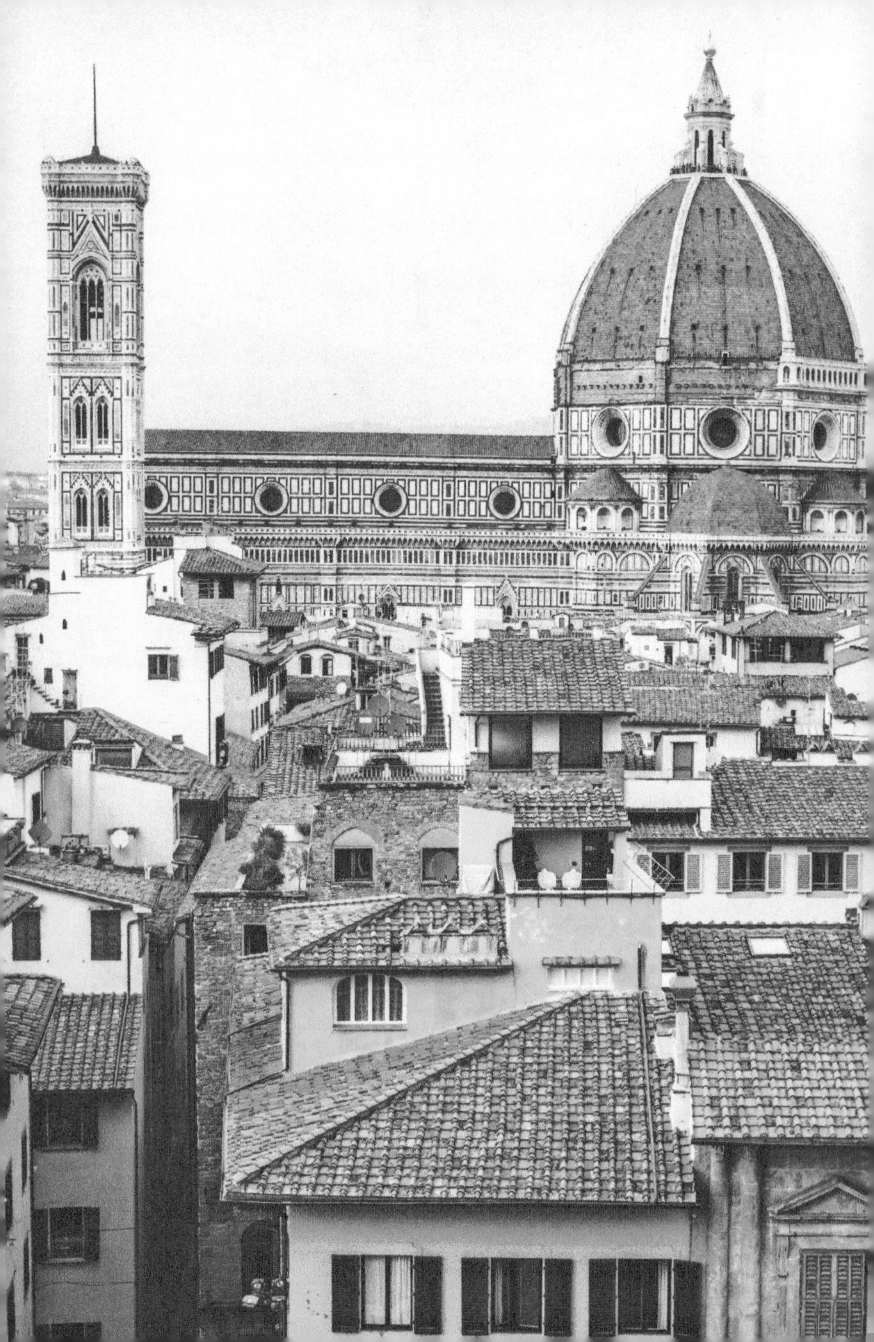

To Know All There Is to Know

The man who never stopped in his pursuit of wisdom

Leonardo da Vinci was born on April 15, 1452, to the notary Piero da Vinci and to a peasant by the name of Caterina. He does not seem to have known his biological mother, but was raised by a loving stepmother, Albiera Amadori, who died when Leonardo was 16. Unlike most well-educated people of the period, he did not learn Latin, Greek, or the canon of classical knowledge until later in life, through his own study. From the beginning, his education was oriented toward the solution of practical problems, even if it was part of Leonardo's genius to understand that, often, such a solution required an understanding of the abstract principles that govern nature.

The Duomo, Florence's main cathedral, was finished in 1436 and remains a symbol of the era that birthed Leonardo—the Italian Renaissance.

The most influential biography of Leonardo is certainly not the most truthful, since it relies on impressions and judgments. But it was instrumental in solidifying the basic themes of what would later become the Leonardo "legend." The renowned painter and foundational figure in the creation of the discipline of art history, Giorgio Vasari, published the first edition of his *Lives of the Most Eminent Painters, Sculptors, and Architects* in 1550, some 31 years after Leonardo's death. Here we find the narrative elements—some true, some false, some still unsubstantiated—that all subsequent biographers would have to confront.

The Birth of a Legend

Vasari tells us that early in the painter's life a peasant came to the home of Leonardo's father with a buckler (a small shield) and asked Ser Piero to have it painted for him in Florence. Leonardo, however, was determined to decorate it so as to "terrify all who should come upon it, producing the same effect as once did the head of Medusa." He surrounded himself with lizards, crickets, serpents, butterflies, grasshoppers, bats, and

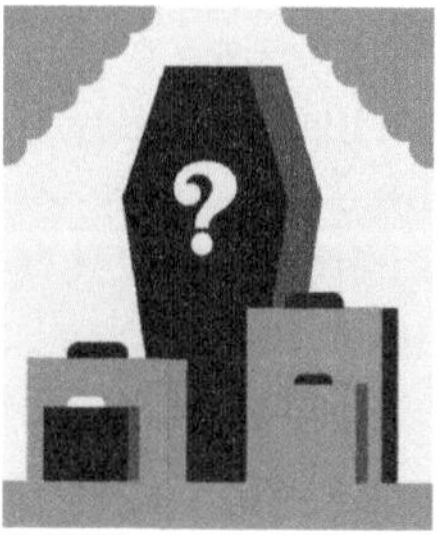

Leonardo was born to an unmarried teenage mother. His father quickly married another teenage girl, who became the principal maternal figure in Leonardo's early life. Yet, decades later, a certain Caterina arrives in Milan and quickly takes up residence in the home of Leonardo, alongside the young protégé Salaì and other men. Two years later Leonardo will pay considerable sums of money for Caterina's funeral, whoever she may have been.

other little creatures, and depicted their likenesses on the wood, alongside that of imaginary creatures breathing smoke from their nostrils and emitting fire from their eyes. He labored so long, Vasari tells us, "that the stench of the dead animals in the room was past bearing, but Leonardo did not notice it, so great was the love he bore towards art."

Such youthful accomplishments motivated Leonardo's father to bring a number of his son's sketches to the great Florentine painter, Andrea del Verrocchio who, in 1466, took Leonardo into his workshop. A decade of apprenticeship and collaboration followed, and eventually the student surpassed the master. It is from this period that we have the earliest known drawing from the artist's hand: a sketch of the Arno valley landscape, most likely dated 1473.

In 1476, Leonardo was accused of sodomy with a local male prostitute, Jacopo Saltarelli. Leonardo was one of four young men denounced—the list included a member of the prominent Tornabuoni family, which enjoyed close relations with the powerful Medici family. The charges were ultimately

Did You Know

Leonardo left little trace of his experiences in childhood. One sharp memory he did relate was of a bird that, as he recalled it, landed on his cradle, forced Leonardo's mouth open with its tail, and struck him on his open mouth repeatedly. Sigmund Freud would later make much of this reminiscence. In Freud's 1910 essay, "A Childhood Memory of Leonardo da Vinci," the author interpreted this memory as an expression of the artist's repressed homosexuality.

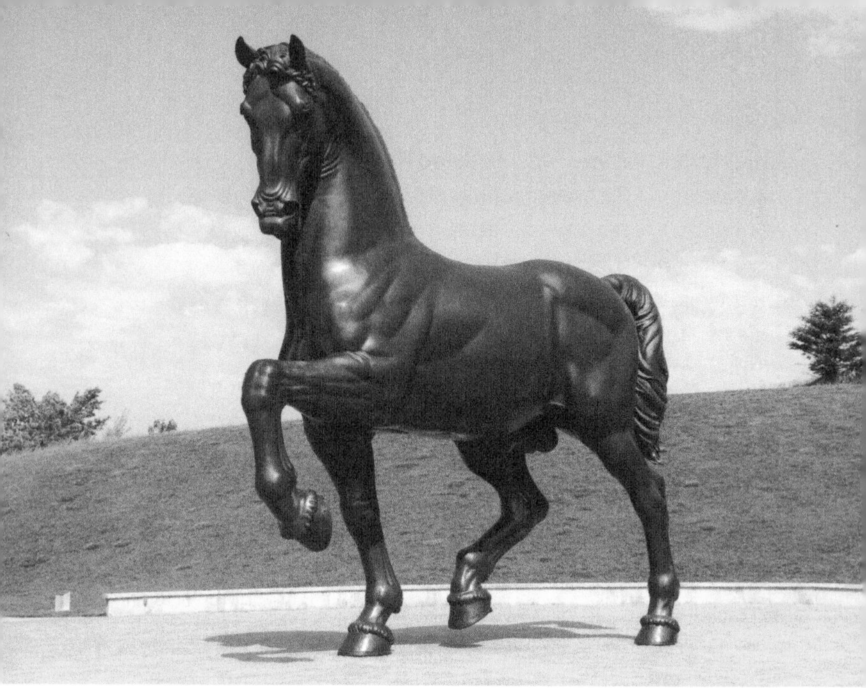

Nina Akamu's 24-foot American Horse *sculpture, located in Michigan, is based on Leonardo's prototype for an unrealized Sforza Monument.*

dismissed, but if they had stuck they could have resulted in any number of punishments, including death.

Nothing is known of Leonardo for the following two years. By 1480 he was likely working under the patronage of Lorenzo de' Medici at the Florence Garden of the Piazza San Marco. There reigned the spirit of Neoplatonism. This current of thought, which had begun to flourish in Renaissance Italy through authors such as Marsilio Ficino and Giovanni Pico della Mirandola, valued the transcendent causes of the things of nature above all, and in turn saw things themselves as mere imitations or reflections of the perfect ideas of them.

A hint of Neoplatonism may indeed be detected in Vasari's description of Leonardo's approach to his work: "It is clear that Leonardo, through his comprehension of art, began many things and never finished one of them, since it seemed to him that the hand was not able to attain the perfection of art in carrying out the things which he imagined." Vasari alternates in his attribution of Leonardo's unfinished projects between loftiness and capriciousness. All of these activities Vasari places under the banner of "philosophizing," and here again we see the dual character of curiosity: it is a sign that one is driven to find the hidden causes of things and understand them in relation to the entire order of creation, but it is also a sign that one is "capricious," distracted, and restless.

Complex Loyalties

In 1482, Lorenzo de' Medici sent Leonardo to make peace with Ludovico Sforza, the duke of Milan, who would become one of Leonardo's most long-lasting patrons. Before the trip, Leonardo wrote a letter to the duke in which he boasts of all the machines he can make to benefit the Milanese: pontoons, scaling ladders, cannons, catapults, and mangonels. He mentions, in passing, that he can paint, and speaks of the commission to build a great bronze horse, "which shall endue with immortal glory and eternal honor the auspicious memory of your father and of the illustrious house of Sforza." This project would weigh on Leonardo throughout much of his life. In 1494, just at the moment when the bronze was to be cast, the Great Italian Wars began, and the valuable metal that would have been used for casting was instead seized and turned into weaponry.

Did You Know

Leonardo was left-handed and wrote from right to left, rather than from left to right, so his letters appear backwards, as if they were being reflected in a mirror. When writing to others, he would force himself to give up this idiosyncrasy so that they could read him. It is not clear whether he invented this shorthand in order to conceal the meaning of his private writings (unlikely, since decryption is simple), or whether it was the result of some innate cognitive disposition.

The Italian Wars would determine the course of Leonardo's life over the next several years. From 1494 to 1559, the Italian city-states were constantly either at war with each other or defending themselves against outside aggressors. His talents as a military engineer and iconic artist meant that, in spite of having worked for their enemies in the past, new regimes always welcomed him. In 1499, Sforza was chased from power by the invading French army under the leadership of Louis XII, and Leonardo found himself, briefly, without a patron, although this did not stop him from providing illustrations for Luca Pacioli's *On Divine Proportion*. In 1502, on the recommendation of Niccolò Machiavelli, Cesare Borgia became his new patron, with whom he would travel as chief military engineer. In this role Leonardo would, among other things, produce a number of innovative maps, and direct the construction of a major canal from the inland city of Cesena to the nearest seaport.

Over the next few years Leonardo traveled extensively and worked on a variety of projects, from canal building to human anatomy. In 1512, King Francis I of France came to Milan, and Leonardo was charged with planning the ceremonial welcome. Vasari evocatively describes the scene as follows: "Leonardo being asked to devise some bizarre thing, made a lion which walked several steps and then opened its breast, and showed it full of lilies." Francis was impressed, and he arranged for Leonardo to return to France with him (along with the *Mona Lisa*, which remains there still). Under French patronage, the artist would spend the last years of his life organizing lavish royal *fêtes*. The philosopher and aesthete had many roles, among them that of a larger-than-life party planner.

Leonardo died at the castle of Clos Lucé in Amboise on May 2, 1519. If Vasari is to be believed, the king of France held Leonardo in his arms as he drew his last breaths.

Leonardo was never able to discover the ultimate truths he sought, nor to see or perceive directly the objects of his most profound contemplation. Vasari returns to the subject of Leonardo's concern with transcendence in his account of the painting of *The Last Supper.* To the heads of the apostles, Vasari writes, Leonardo "gave such majesty and beauty, that he left the head of Christ unfinished, not believing that he was able to give it that divine air which is essential to the image of Christ."

In this painting, perhaps, lies the epitome of Leonardo's life and work. Driven to know and to depict all of nature and its beings with perfection, Leonardo knew in the end that he was only aspiring, searching after things that lay beyond his grasp, that could not be known or perceived or depicted directly, but merely hinted at. It was a partial life: a life of desire, sublimated into curiosity, forever unquenched.

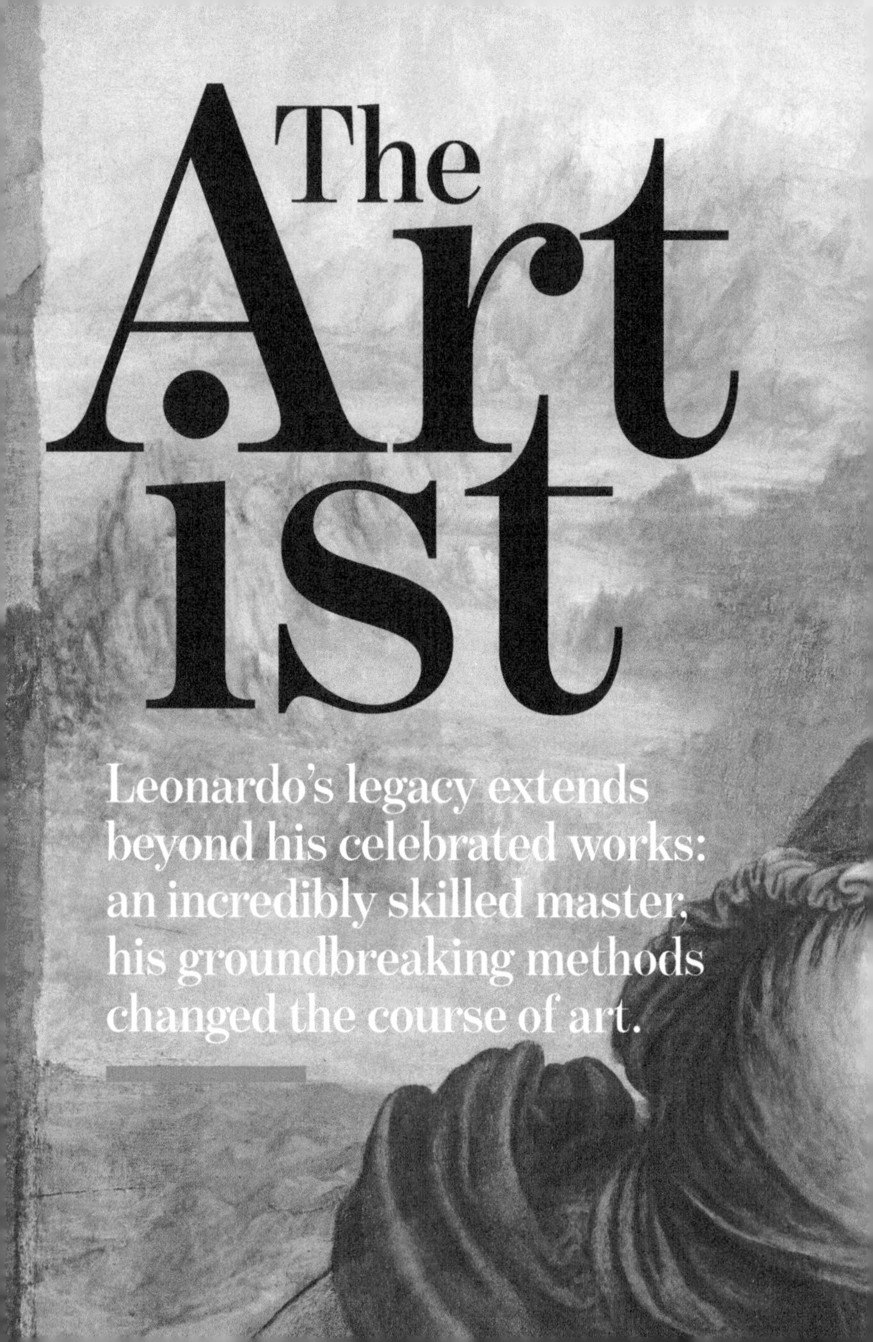

The Artist

Leonardo's legacy extends beyond his celebrated works: an incredibly skilled master, his groundbreaking methods changed the course of art.

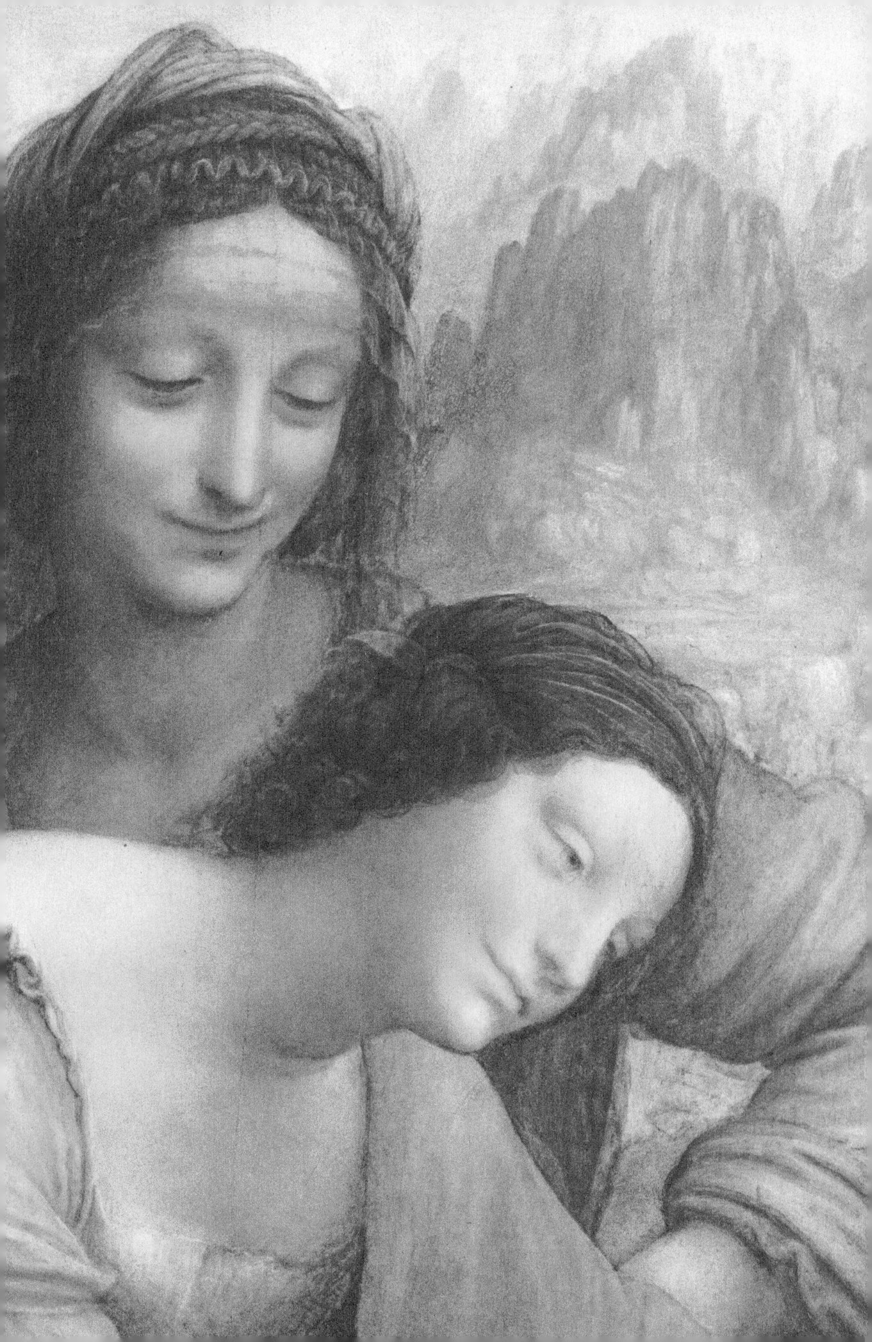

Leonardo was guided in all of his endeavors by a firm belief in the unity of what we today call "art" and "science." His paintings and drawings were, among other things, studies in the nature of perception, the properties of light, and the structure of the natural world. They were meant to be beautiful, of course, but nature itself was for Leonardo intrinsically beautiful; the ultimate purpose of figurative art was to reflect or to transmit this beauty—not to usurp nature, but to harmonize one's perceptions perfectly to it.

Nowhere is this harmony more evident than in his anatomical illustrations, which are meant to capture the wonder of the human bodily "machine," whilst simultaneously aiding the advancement of medicine. In addition to his innovations in the representation of human and animal anatomy, his other great contribution lies in the representation of spatial perspective and light. For Leonardo, perspective could be established from any number of possible points of view—a break with the dominant school of thought during his time. Moreover, perspective is not just a matter of the representation of spatial position but, also, of light and color; thus, for Leonardo, the representation of perspective in painting must be informed not only by geometry but also by geometrical optics. For example, he noticed that objects in the distance appear bluer or darker, an observation that Leonardo utilizes to great effect in *Virgin of the Rocks*.

According to Leon Battista Alberti, an influential painter and author who wrote extensively on composition theory during the Renaissance, "Mathematicians measure with their minds alone the forms of things separated from all matter." The painter, by contrast, "is concerned solely with representing what can be seen," and "has nothing to do with things that are not visible." Yet the work of the painter builds and depends upon the work of the mathematician, because what can be seen is in the end supported or underlain by invisible forms whose properties can be known only by means of mathematics. Leonardo evidently conceived of his work as that of a painter and a mathematician at once. He understood the importance of the mathematical principles of form for the compelling depiction of physical reality, and in the deeper sense that representation of perceptible things is a step on the way to the contemplation and appreciation of the principles behind reality.

Art Not for Art's Sake

To the extent that Leonardo da Vinci conceived his life's work as that of an "artist," he does not seem to have thought of painting as his primary or preferred medium, despite the implied objections of the throngs at the Louvre. A young apprentice working at a work-shop such as Verrocchio's and hoping

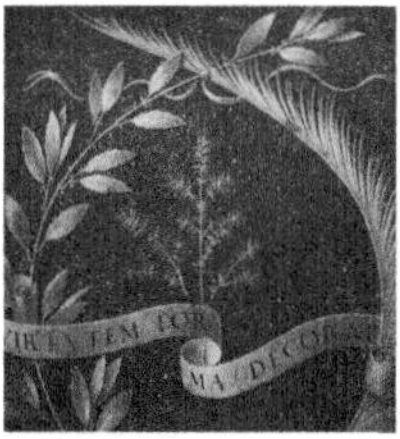

Visual Games

Leonardo often played with traditional iconography and symbolism. Sometimes his symbols were more focused on the individual circumstances of the painting. Thus on the reverse side of his portrait of Ginevra de' Benci (c. 1474–78) he includes a sprig of juniper (in Italian, *ginepro*), which evokes the name of the girl sitting for the painting. The sprig is flanked by laurel and palm, and around it runs a banner with the Latin motto *Virtutem forma decorat* ("Beauty adorns virtue").

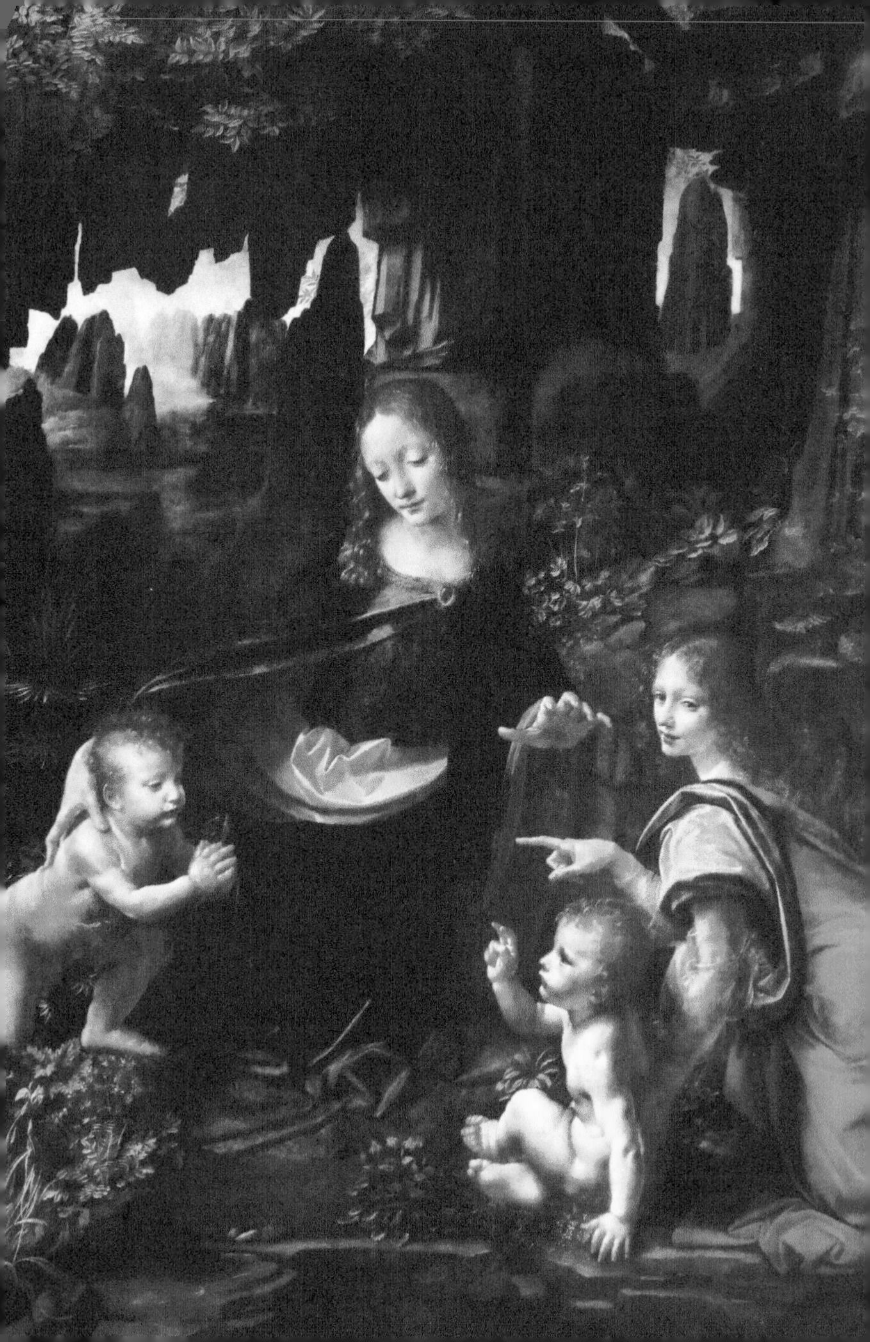

to receive noble patronage, would be required to demonstrate competence in numerous media, not least painting and statuary but, also, in the decorative arts and architecture. If paintings are better known than other artistic works of Leonardo's, it may simply be because they are easier to preserve than sculptures or buildings.

Though stylistically innovative, his paintings are rooted in tradition, and the subjects are fairly limited. Of the 22 paintings that are incontrovertibly Leonardo's, 14 focus on biblical subjects (8 of these on the Virgin Mary), and one on a hagiographical tale. The remaining seven are portraits, six of those of women. There is a further painting on a mythological theme, that of Leda and the swan, which was reproduced by Leonardo's protégé Francesco Melzi around 1508–15, but was subsequently lost.

But it would be erroneous to judge the innovativeness of Leonardo da Vinci's paintings in terms of their content, for this overlooks the far more important dimensions of technique, style, and sensibility applied on familiar themes. His contributions to perspective and to geometrical optics, the study of the role of light and color in spatial perspective, his intense attention to the phenomenal qualities of his own visual perception, yielded important innovations in the use of pigments. The use of rich blue to highlight spatial depth in the *Virgin of the Rocks* (left); his careful attention to the qualities of statuary; his ability to paint (as in the *Madonna with a Cardinal* or the *Benois Madonna*) the folds of fabric in a way that evokes the three-dimensional quality of sculpture—all these accomplishments betray a sort of interdisciplinary mastery in one art form through excellence in another.

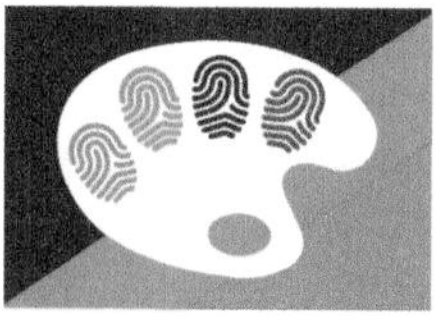

On a few canvases, faint traces of fingerprints have been detected. One of the most striking appearances of this deeply personal signature of the artist is found on *The Baptism of Christ* (c. 1470–75), where his prints are visible in the flesh of Jesus.

For Leonardo, the supreme goal of painting is to represent the world as it in fact appears to us, but not in a realist sense. He is not simply recording what he sees, but giving testimony of an intense free play of the imagination. He represents nature as it is, but it is a nature charged with his own sense of fantasia, a mix of styles and techniques brought together through personal improvisation. This is particularly evident in the landscapes in the background, showing sharp precipices and dark forests that seem to anticipate the German Romanticism of the late 18th century more than they embody the aesthetic sensibility of the Italian Renaissance.

Reading His Work Visually

Also close to fantasia is Leonardo's creative use of iconography in order to convey subtle ideas about his subjects. In the *Madonna Litta,* the baby Jesus holds an almost imperceptible finch, a common Renaissance symbol of passion, while the *Lady with an Ermine* (see p. 39), a portrait of the Duke of Milan's new mistress, associates her character to the animal that is supposedly so pure it would rather die than soil its perfect white coat. Sometimes the richness of a symbol extends well beyond its traditional interpretation. In the *Benois Madonna,* Mary holds up the small stalk of a plant with two cruciform purple flowers.

The baby Jesus inspects the specimen with intense curiosity. Is he contemplating his own future crucifixion? This might be a common interpretation, but it seems to overlook what we know of the artist. The baby is tending to a small instance of the order of nature, he is taking it in with his eyes, absorbing it. It is a sensual activity, and it is the sort of activity that defined the artist's own life: the intense contemplation of the visible properties of natural things in the knowledge of their instantiation of divine order. One detects here, indeed, a small hint of autobiography.

Leonardo's late work *The Virgin and Child with St. Anne* (see p. 41), merits special attention, as it combines and perfects most of these techniques. It was painted beginning around 1510, on wood, and today hangs on the wall of the main hall of the Denon Wing of the Louvre, outside the "*Mona Lisa* Room." While the relationship between Mary; her mother, Anne; and the Christ child is a common theme in Renaissance art, Leonardo upends some of the usual conventions of their representation. Notably, he places Mary directly on her mother's lap, both of them sitting barefoot and

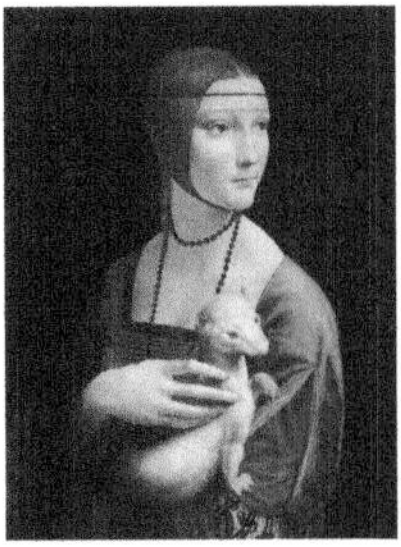

Startled Ermine

***Lady with an Ermine* (c. 1489–90) marked an innovation in portrait painting.** The woman, likely Cecilia Gallerani, seems to be responding to a sudden happening beyond the frame, presumably the entrance of another person into the room. In real life such a pose, of woman and animal, could not possibly last more than a few seconds. In this way Leonardo has overcome a major limitation in earlier portraiture.

at ease. Anne peers down happily at Mary; the latter looks longingly at her son, who in turn is looking back at his mother. There is a fourth character, unnamed in the title of the painting but no less important for its symmetry and role: it is a small lamb, looking up at Jesus. The animal replaces the young St. John the Baptist, much more often depicted in connection with these other figures. For example, the so-called *Burlington House Cartoon*, drawn some years earlier in 1499 or 1500, also shows Mary, again on Anne's lap, but Jesus in turn on Mary's lap, as John the Baptist leans in. In the painting with the lamb, all four beings form a pyramid, with the lamb in a bottom corner and Anne's head at the summit. Anne appears as young as her daughter, and both are beautiful, yet seemingly unrelated. Mary wears a blue robe that matches, and seems to have emerged from, the fantastical icy mountain scene in the deep background. A lone, dark, and massive tree stands to the right in the middle background. The scene synthesizes reality and unreality perhaps more successfully than any of his other paintings: Mary seems no less real, no less a historical person, than *La Gioconda*. Unlike *La Gioconda*, however, she is surrounded by others, and sensuous and fleshy love swirls around them. The tableau functions simultaneously as a

> *He is not simply recording what he sees, but giving testimony of an intense free play of the imagination.*

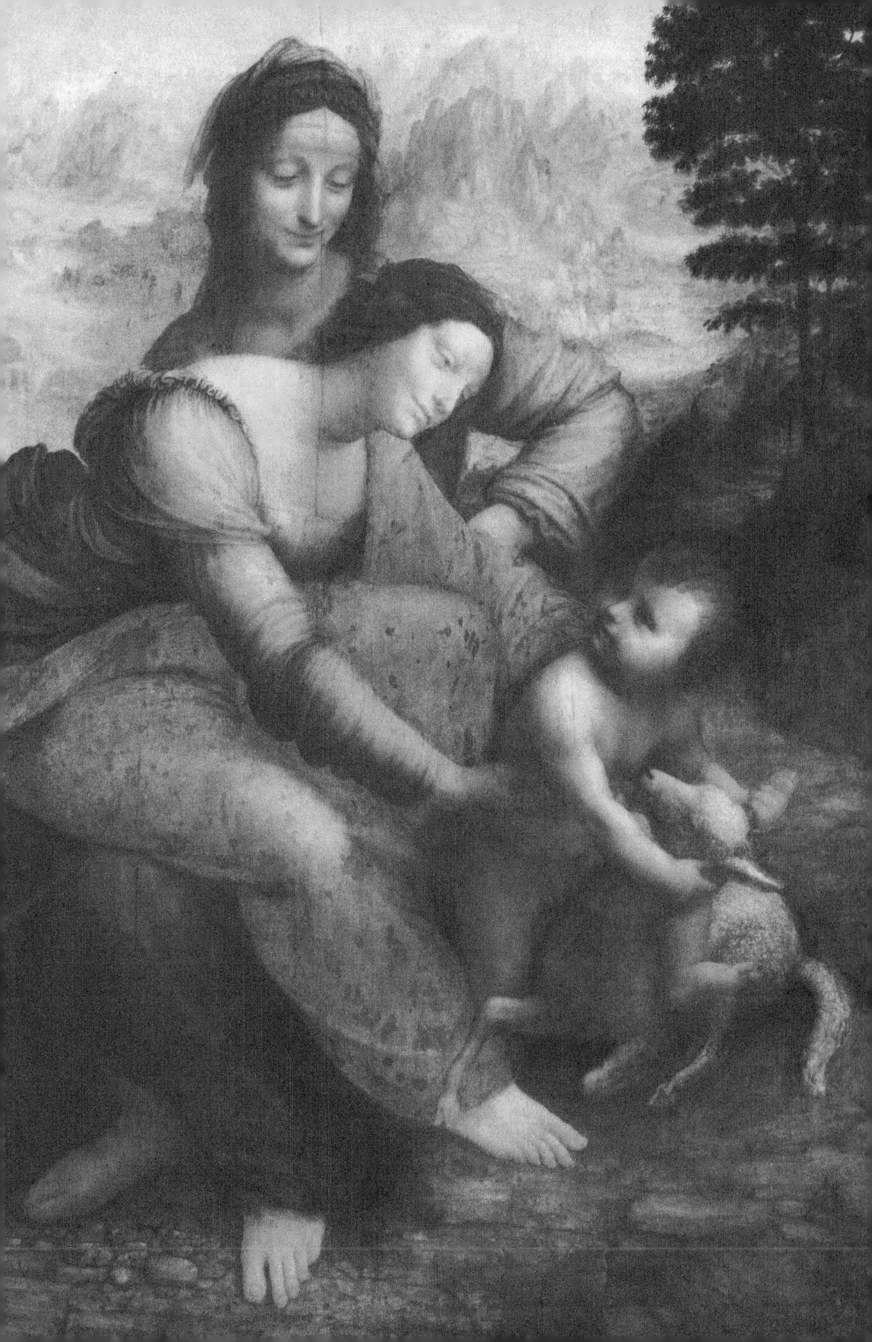

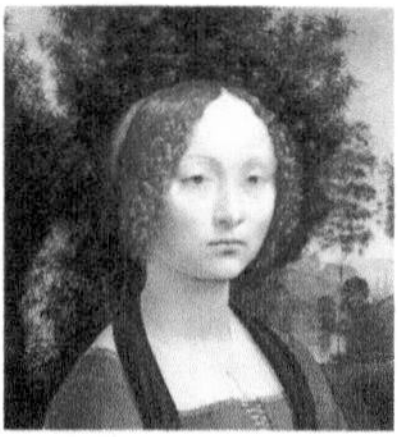

Trade Tools

Leonardo was the master of the technique called *sfumato*, which literally means "smoked," and alongside *cangiante* ("changing"), *chiaroscuro* ("light-dark"), and *unione* ("union"), is considered one of the four basic modes of Renaissance painting. The power of his best-known portraits (see above) arises from his use of this technique to tone down or to gradually dissipate the surface of a face or body into what lies beyond it, so as to do entirely without lines and borders in some cases.

symbolic register, as well; with symbols both clear and opaque, it is evidently intent on saying something other than, simply, "Here is a manifest instance of human (and creaturely) love." The scene depicts something mysterious, in the way that the birth of Jesus is itself mysterious: impossible by standard means of accounting, inexplicable by the ordinary laws of nature. As a painter, Leonardo respected these laws; they were the basis of all of his work, but he was intent on piercing into what lay behind them—doing, that is, what Alberti had asserted painters do not do. In *The Virgin and Child with St. Anne*, he may well have succeeded in this.

Leonardo's late work, *St. John the Baptist* (see p. 59), likely painted between 1513 and 1516, contains numerous allusions to other works of the artist, and in many ways seems like a culmination of them. It shows a single figure, alone yet still conveying the sort of sensuous joy we see in the depiction of Mary and her family just described. St. John the Baptist is

Tempera A painting technique originally involving the use of egg yolk to permanently attach pigment to a surface.

pointing upwards toward heaven, announcing the coming of Christ, but also completing a gesture made by St. Anne's unfinished hand in the *Burlington House Cartoon,* which served as an anticipatory study for *The Virgin and Child with St. Anne*. He is androgynous, as St. John the Baptist often is in Renaissance painting, and in fact seems to combine the features of two characters that Leonardo had already studied. One is his servant and protégé, Salaì, who, as Vasari will later relate, "was most comely in grace and beauty, having fine locks, curling in ringlets, in which Leonardo greatly delighted." The other is *Mona Lisa*, more properly known as Lisa Gherardini, wife of Francesco del Giocondo. Lisa is given a sumptuous landscape of trees and lakes behind her, whereas St. John the Baptist is, so to speak, pure *sfumato*: His features fade only into black, a black that absorbs the rest of the canvas. But he shares the same deep apricot flesh, and, most tellingly, he shares the same smile.

He smiles, like Lisa, but it is not an entirely affirmative smile. There is something vaguely dishonest about his expression, something we sense could ensnare us if we let it hold our attention for too long. He channels, and perfects, so many of the great instances of beauty from Leonardo da Vinci's earlier life. Real or unreal, contemporary or biblical or mythological, his subjects reveal themselves to be avatars of one another, united, at least, in beauty.

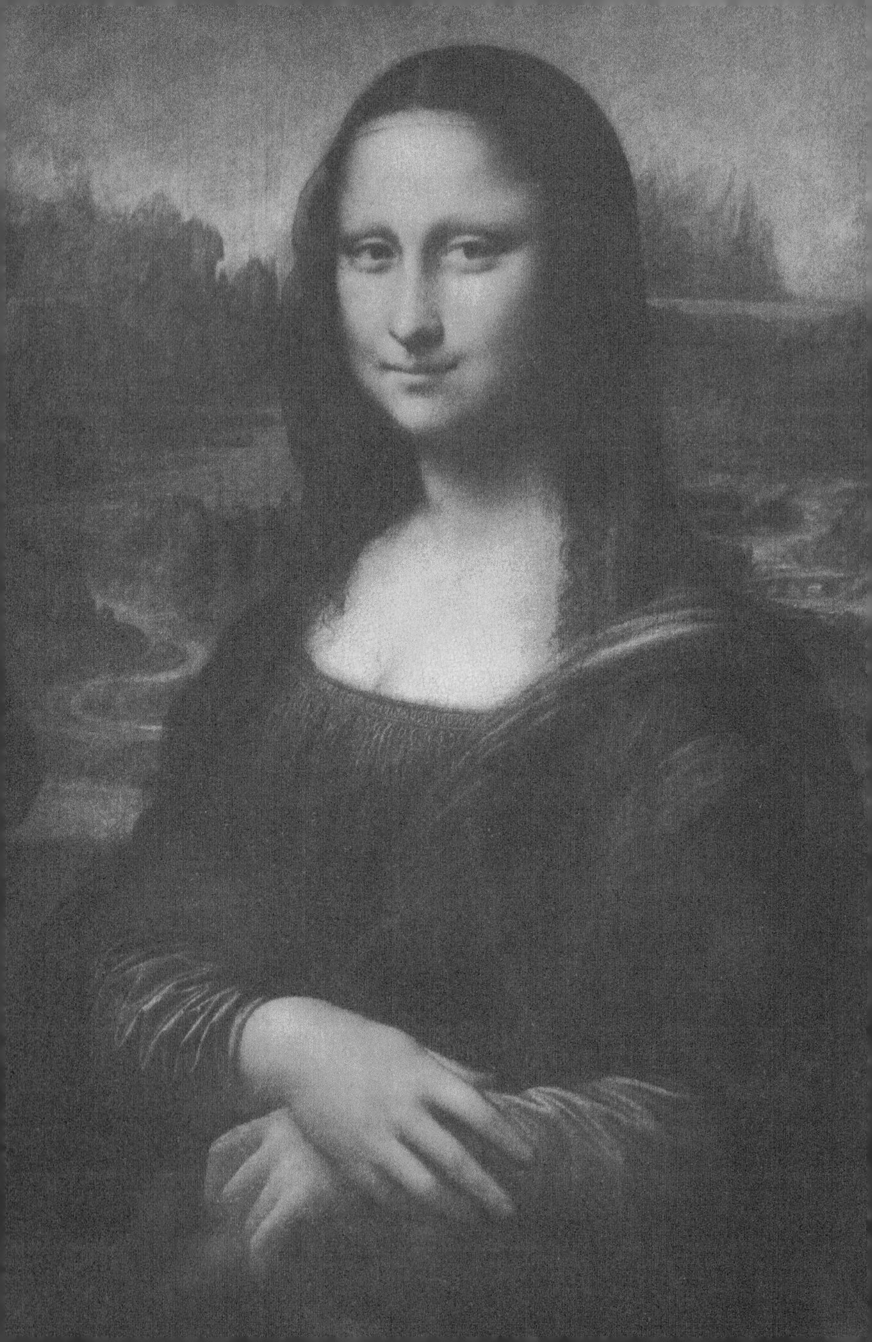

Gioconda's Smile

What gives the *Mona Lisa* its iconic power

It is said that when Lisa Gherardini sat for her portrait, some time between 1503 and 1507, the master painter arranged to have jugglers and jesters performing behind him as he worked, so that she would maintain the happy expression that would later consolidate her celebrity.

Did he understand at that time what he was bringing into the world? Of course not. The future value of a work of art is beyond the power of any individual to predict. Yet Leonardo da Vinci may well have sensed that something new was being born, something that hinted at the coming of a world that was no longer a reiteration of the past, but was, rather, loyal to the individual human being, with her or his quirks, passing moods, happy moments, and ordinary, everyday joys. This was the beginning of the modern era: the cult of the individual, the launching of superstars from nothing more than a fleeting grin. Lisa Gherardini's fame, like the fame of all her descendants in the cult of celebrity, derives simply from her being herself.

Lisa Gherardini was born in June 1479, putting her in her mid-to-late twenties at the time she sat for Leonardo. She came from a prosperous Florentine family, which had made most of its wealth through farming wheat and producing wine and olive oil. The Gherardini family was distinguished and deeply rooted in the region, and the surname carried weight. By the time she married Francesco del Giocondo in 1495 at the age of 15, her family's fortunes had mostly dried up, so the marriage combined her old name with his new wealth. The couple had five children together, and she lived to a considerably old age. All indications suggest that she led a happy life, and probably smiled frequently.

I'll Be Your Mirror

Smiles can be interpreted in many ways. In the 16th century, her portrayal conveyed conventional signals of virtue—notably, by placing the right hand over the left. Much later, over the course of the 19th century, her gaze would be seen as seductive and she would be recast as a femme fatale. This is the interpretation that gives life to the 1950 Nat King Cole song "Mona Lisa." "Do you smile to tempt a lover, Mona Lisa?" asks the singer. The answer is, of course, no. If this were her message, then the signal would have been definitively cancelled out by her virtuous and monogamous hand-crossing.

It was only recently, in 2005, that Lisa Gherardini's identity emerged, when a note written in 1503 by the Florentine clerk Agostino Vespucci naming her was found. In some respects, this positive identification raises more questions than it answers—and, in fact, there is an ongoing dispute over its

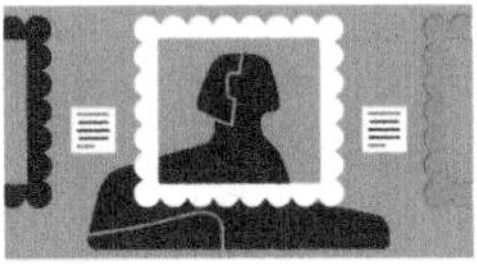

After returning from his Egyptian campaign in 1799, the soon-to-be emperor of France, Napoleon, found himself captivated by the *Mona Lisa*, and referred to her as the "Sphinx of the Occident."

veracity. If the painting was commissioned for del Giocondo as a private matter, it is not clear why Leonardo brought it with him, as he seems to have done, when he left for France around 1515. We know that when the painter died a few years later he left it to Salaì. King Francis I bought the *Mona Lisa* from Salaì and kept it at Fontainebleau, where it remained until Louis XIV had it moved to Versailles in the 17th century. It came to its current home at the Louvre only after the French Revolution, and nearly since its arrival it has been the supreme example of state-owned art.

Revered, Reviled

As with all celebrities, the *Mona Lisa*'s preciousness in part explains the long victimization she has endured at the hands of satirists, vandals, and even kidnappers. Guillaume Apollinaire, the French poet who coined the term "surrealism," often spoke of how he would like to see the Louvre burned to the ground. When the *Mona Lisa* was stolen by the Italian thief Vincenzo Peruggia in 1911, purportedly for "patriotic" reasons, Apollinaire was taken into police custody for questioning. He implicated his friend Pablo Picasso. Both were eventually released for lack of evidence, and Peruggia was arrested two years later while attempting to turn the painting over, for a "reward," to a gallery in its hometown of Florence. But the very idea that the Cubists might have been to blame shows something of the rift that was taking place, and of the symbolic charge the *Mona Lisa* had developed. While the most famous satirical riffs on the sincere depiction of her smile would come some decades later—with Marcel Duchamp's mustachioed *Mona Lisa* of 1965 (right), and Andy Warhol's various lithographic multiplications of her likeness. In fact, she had already been lampooned just a few years after Leonardo's death when Salaì painted the so-called *Nude Gioconda*, depicting a bare-breasted woman who looks somewhat like Lisa Gherardini, but even more so like Salaì himself.

It has been obvious, then, since the late 19th century, that the *Mona Lisa*, unaltered, unmolested, is considered, in the art world, supremely uncool. She represents what so many would have liked to burn down, or at least what they would have liked to replace with their own purportedly more vital productions. Parallel to this development in the art world, we see in the broader popular culture a simultaneous and unsurprising commodification. At just the same time that Georges Bataille, Duchamp, and others create their own works out of the desecration of the *Mona Lisa*, capitalism, too, makes tremendous profits out of the reproduction of Leonardo's painting on

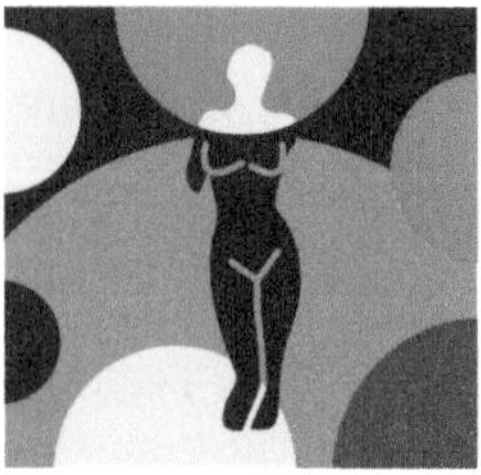

Coincidence? The 1503 marginal note of Agostino Vespucci, identifying Lisa Gherardini as the subject of the painting, was written next to a passage in a copy of Cicero's *Epistolae ad familiares*, in which the Roman philosopher and orator mentions that the Greek painter Apelles had depicted the body of Venus with less detail than the head and shoulders.

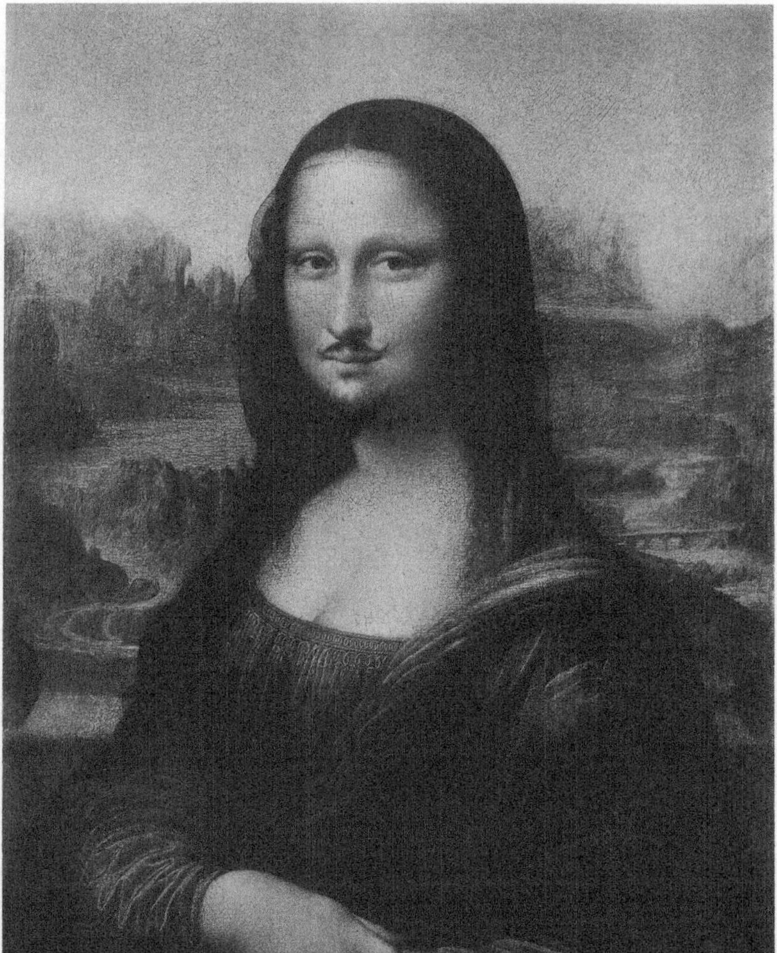

L. H. O. O. Q.

Marcel Duchamp (réplique 1930)

T-shirts, coffee mugs, calendars, and basically any surface that permits the image to be seared onto it and then sold, at considerably less value than the original, to modern secular pilgrims.

Whether it's Warhol or the lowliest souvenir vendor, the 20th century learned how to cash in on the *Mona Lisa*'s celebrity status. But like any mega-celebrity, she would come to represent, potentially, all things to all people. And, inevitably, just as Hollywood stars are sent on political missions to represent causes they sometimes understand no better than your average citizen, so too in the 20th century, the *Mona Lisa* was transformed into an international diplomat. In January 1963 she was sent on loan to the National Gallery of Art in Washington, DC. A period news report informs us that the unloading was "accompanied by all the security measures reserved for visiting heads of state." President Kennedy gave her a grand ceremonial welcome. In his prepared speech for the occasion, he described the painting as "the second lady that the people of France have sent to the United States," and he assured the American people that "though she will not stay with us

Did You Know

King Francis I hung the *Mona Lisa* in his en-suite bathroom at the Palace at Fontainebleau, along with other artworks. These works would eventually migrate to Versailles with Louis XIV, and then to the Louvre, where they would serve as the core of what would later become the largest public art display in the world. There was no expectation that the work would ever become as popular as it is today, but it is noteworthy that of all the paintings at the Louvre, the one that is most beloved is also the oldest, and had been invested with such great expectations by its first owner.

as long as the Statue of Liberty, our appreciation is equally great." But the 1886 gift that stands in New York Harbor was meant to stand for something specific, indeed something distinctly American that the statue's French creators valued. How could a private portrait of an ordinary woman painted in the Renaissance possibly be compared to this? Kennedy carried on, referring to the painting as "this great creation of the civilization which we share, the beliefs which we protect, and the aspirations toward which we together strive." But the more rhetoric was added, the more tenuous the symbolic connection to the Statue of Liberty appeared.

Kennedy was, as they say, "politicizing" a cultural artifact. The moment Leonardo painted the *Mona Lisa*, she took on a political life, as all cultural objects do. She signaled the power of the family for which she was made, the maneuvering and strategizing that always play into the patronage of the arts, and the immortalizing, in portraits, of moderately influential men and their wives. But this political significance was certainly worlds away from the one the American president would later project onto it.

The *Mona Lisa* is exposed as a cipher; a romantic cliché for songwriters; a joke for avant-garde artists; a quick buck for merchandisers; and, for the president of the United States, a symbol of freedom, enlightenment, and, implicitly, the superiority of the American model over Soviet Communism in the Cold War. When Lisa Gherardini sat patiently for Leonardo, she could not possibly have imagined what her small smile would later be made to do. Or, perhaps, watching the fools and jugglers go about their work as Leonardo went about his, she was actually able to glimpse some small trace of what was to come—and smiled.

TIMELINE

THE LADY ON TOUR

THE *MONA LISA* IS ONE OF THE MOST WELL-TRAVELED PAINTINGS

1514
FRANCIS I INVITES LEONARDO TO FRANCE. The following year, visitors report seeing the *Mona Lisa* among his possessions.

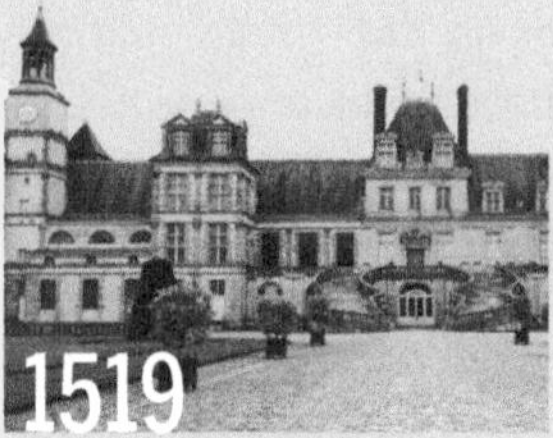

1519
LEONARDO DIES, leaving the painting to Salaì. Soon after, Francis I purchases it, and places it in the castle at Fontainebleau.

1646
LOUIS XIV transfers the painting to Paris.

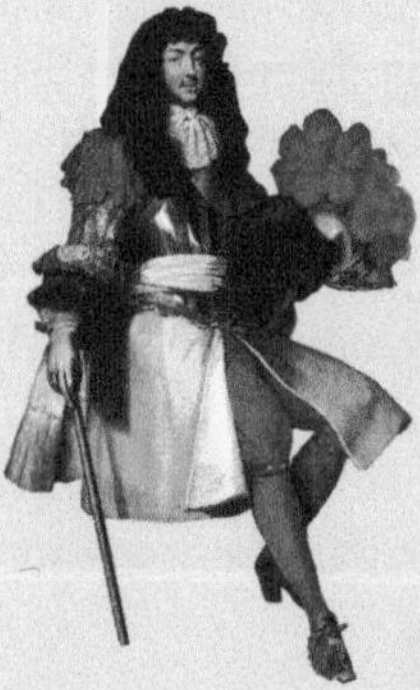

1665
IT MOVES AGAIN from the Palais du Louvre to the nearby Palais des Tuileries.

1690
LOUIS XIV AGAIN transfers the *Mona Lisa* to the Palais de Versailles.

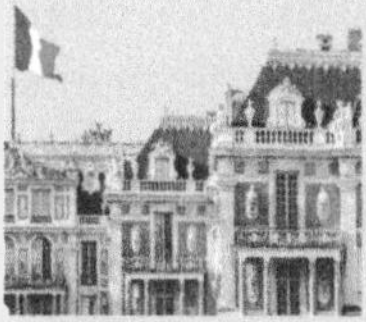

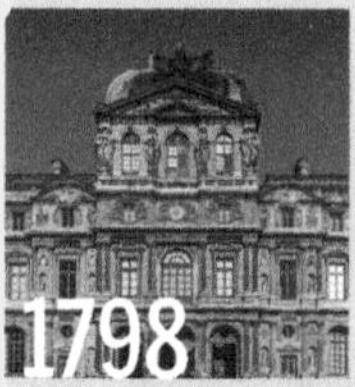

1798
IT MAKES ITS FIRST APPEARANCE at the post-Revolutionary Louvre.

1800
NAPOLEON BONAPARTE takes it to his bedroom at the Palais des Tuileries.

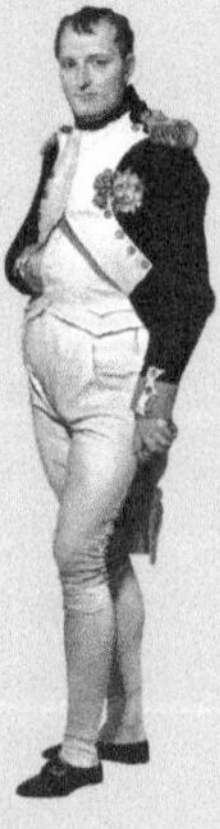

1804

THE *MONA LISA* RETURNS to the Louvre.

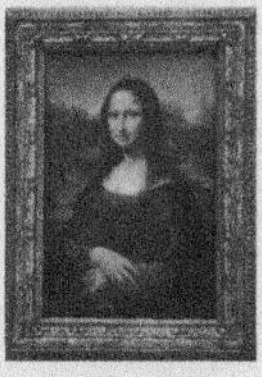

1870

THE PAINTING IS PLACED IN UNDERGROUND STORAGE at the Brest Arsenal for safekeeping during the Franco-Prussian War.

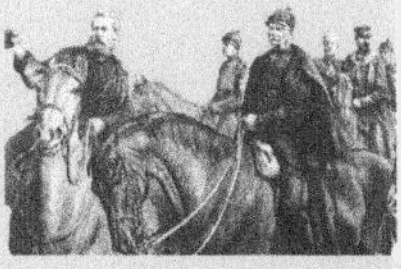

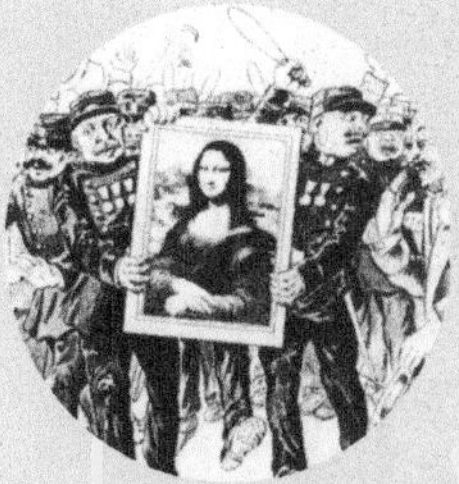

1911

ON AUGUST 20, the Italian worker Vincenzo Peruggia hides in the Louvre and steals the *Mona Lisa* during the night.

1913

THE PAINTING TURNS UP IN FLORENCE, where Peruggia had attempted to pass it on to a local gallery, evidently in exchange for a "reward."

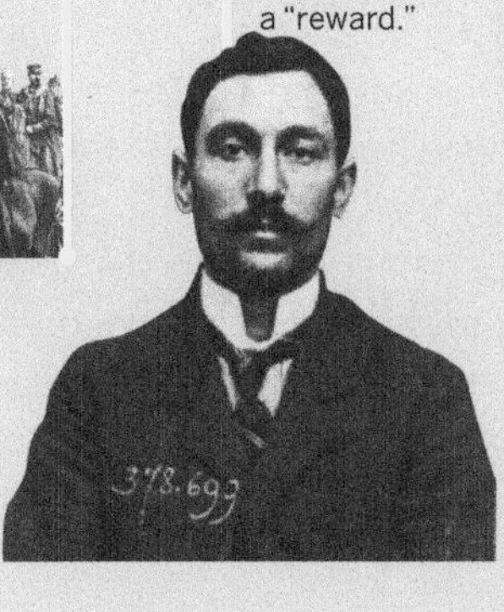

1914–1918

THE *MONA LISA* IS TAKEN to Bordeaux, then to Toulouse, for safekeeping during the war.

1939–1945

IT SPENDS THE WAR YEARS TRAVELING from castle to castle throughout the French countryside.

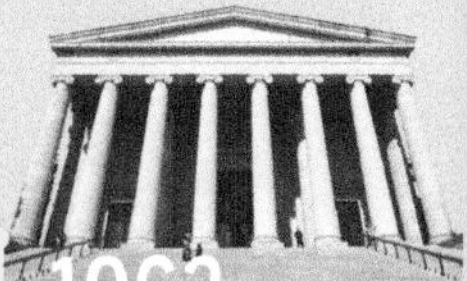

1963

ANDRÉ MALRAUX SENDS THE *MONA LISA* TO THE UNITED STATES, where it is briefly exhibited in the National Gallery in Washington, DC, then at the Metropolitan Museum of Art in New York.

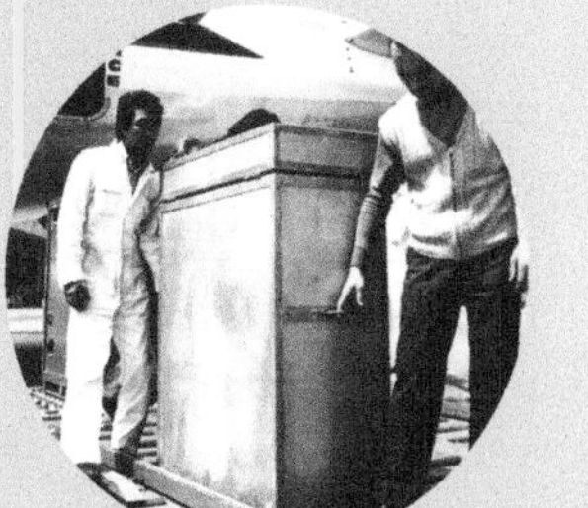

1974

THE MONA LISA IS EXHIBITED in the National Museum of Western Art in Tokyo, and makes a brief appearance in Moscow.

The Economy of Kitsch

THE ORIGINAL MAY BE PRICELESS, BUT *MONA LISA*'S LIKENESS CAN BE HAD FOR AS LITTLE AS ONE DOLLAR

Among the items you may currently purchase bearing the likeness of the *Mona Lisa* are posters, notebooks, coffee mugs, magnets, watches, headphones, fans, pencil pouches, greeting cards, throw pillows, infant onesies, jigsaw puzzles, Rubik's cubes, and paint-by-numbers kits. Many of these feature variations in which *Mona Lisa* is not an ordinary woman, but one wearing sunglasses or a mohawk; one turned into a cat or metamorphosed into a lizard; one portrayed as a Rastifarian, or even as Betty Boop. Music boxes bearing her likeness play the melody of the Nat King Cole tune. You will often see Lisa Gherardini's face featured next to Botticelli's Venus being born from a clamshell, or Raphael's contemplative cherubs. These are images so familiar that we see them, usually, as incitements not to appreciate them as aesthetes, nor to think about them as art critics, but to screen them out (or, depending on circumstances, to buy their mass-produced representations as gifts for our loved ones and as mementos of our own insouciance).

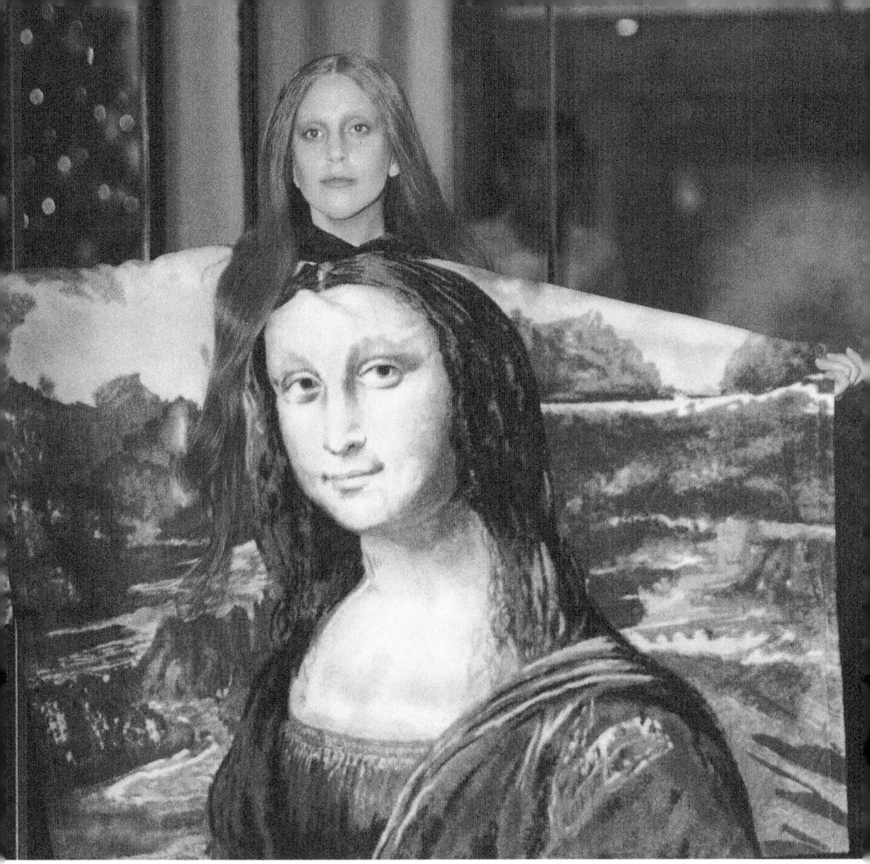

The Mona Lisa*'s timeless smile has been commodified by modern fashion, as seen in pop star Lady Gaga's 2013 outfit.*

But none of this says anything about the images themselves. Leonardo did not mass produce the *Mona Lisa*. He produced one (with perhaps one earlier iteration, the so-called "Isleworth *Mona Lisa*") and he worked on it obsessively for years. He did not make millions of copies, but rather applied millions of gentle strokes to a single copy.

THE LIST

Leonardo's Best-Known Works

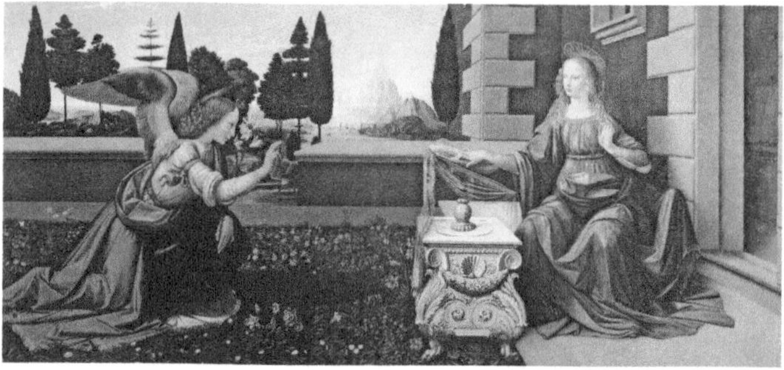

▲ The Annunciation

PAINTED *c. 1473–75*

LOCATED *The Uffizi, Florence*

This painting shows the artist's early fascination with the Virgin Mary, and also his genius for adapting traditional themes to his own original, even strange, vision of the world.

The Adoration of the Magi

PAINTED *c. 1480–81*

LOCATED *The Uffizi, Florence*

The men and animals traditionally calmed by the baby Jesus's presence in the manger have been radically replaced by men thrown to the ground in what looks like stupor, or perhaps wonder.

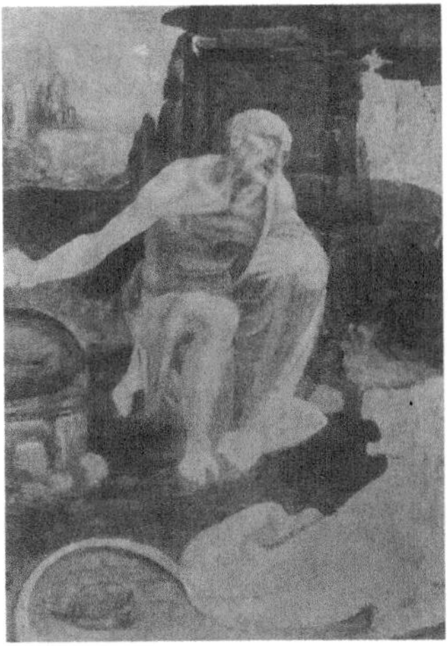

^ St. Jerome in the Wilderness

PAINTED *c. 1480–82*

LOCATED *Museums of the Vatican, Vatican City*

This stark image is focused on the well-known subject of St. Jerome's sojourn in the desert. The flesh of his chest appears remarkably similar to what will later be seen in Leonardo's anatomical studies. Jerome has been made so ascetic as to resemble a corpse.

v Virgin of the Rocks (later version)

PAINTED *c. 1490s*

LOCATED *National Gallery, London*

This work features Mary with the baby Jesus, a young St. John the Baptist, and an angel. A fifth subject, perhaps, is the landscape, a stark scene of jagged rocks and what appear to be grottoes. It is considered Leonardo's most perfect use of *sfumato*.

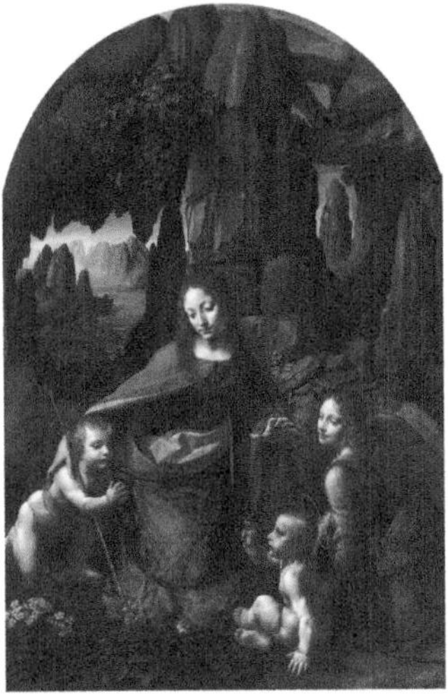

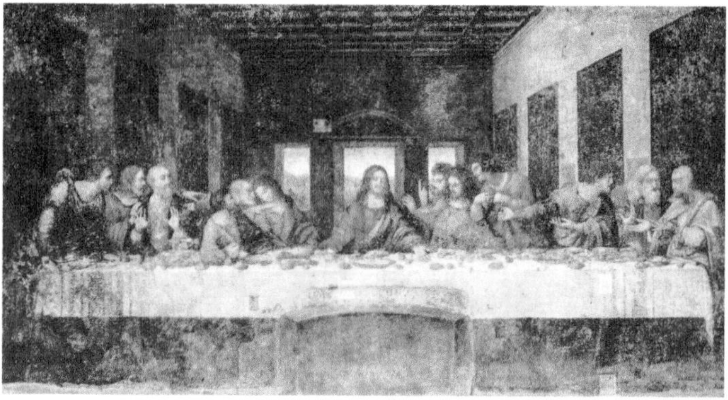

Vitruvian Man

DRAWN *c. 1490*

LOCATED *Galleria dell'Accademia, Venice*

This simple figure, showing a man inscribed in a circle and a square (see p. 105), was meant to show the geometrical proportions of the human body, but over time has come to stand as a symbol of humanity itself.

∧ The Last Supper

PAINTED *c. 1495–97*

LOCATED *Santa Maria delle Grazie, Milan*

Considered the greatest painterly accomplishment during his lifetime, it is still praised for its masterful depiction of perspective: the room retreating to the horizon behind the diners, suspended between the human and the divine, death and life.

∨ Mona Lisa

PAINTED *c. 1503–7*

LOCATED *The Louvre, Paris*

Though the subject of this painting had her own, small, human existence, she would come to represent something far larger: not so much humanity itself, but something toward which humanity aspires.

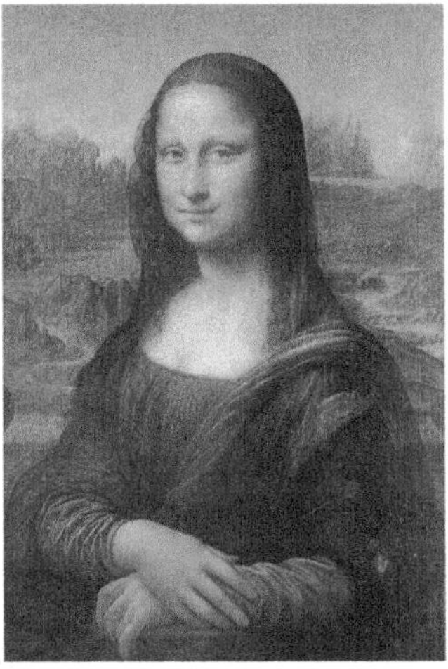

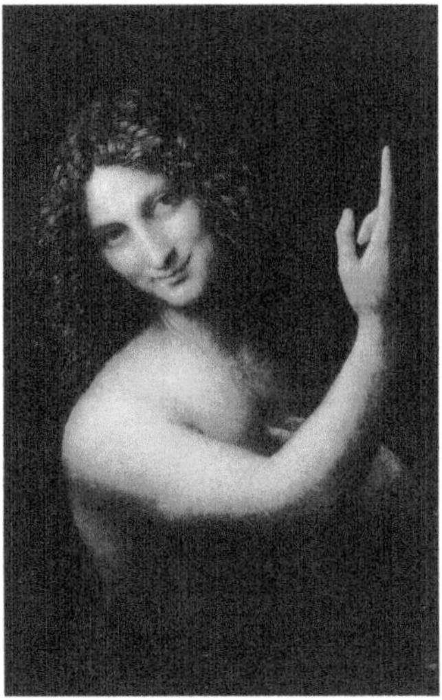

∧ St. John the Baptist

PAINTED *c. 1513–16*

LOCATED *The Louvre, Paris*

The late St. John the Baptist offers a fine contrast to Leonardo's early St. Jerome: as fleshy as his predecessor was haggard, as mischievous as his predecessor was pure of heart. The likely true subject of this portrait is not a saint at all, but a "devil": the young Salaì.

The Invent

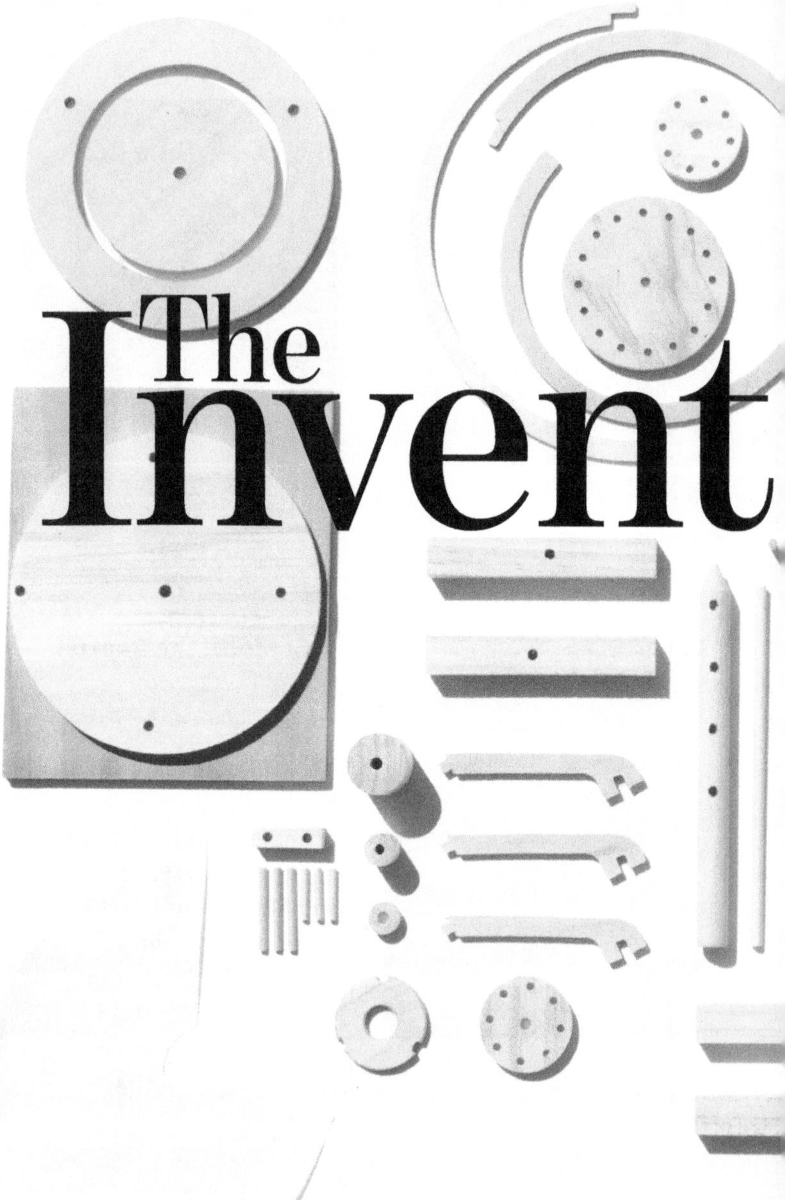

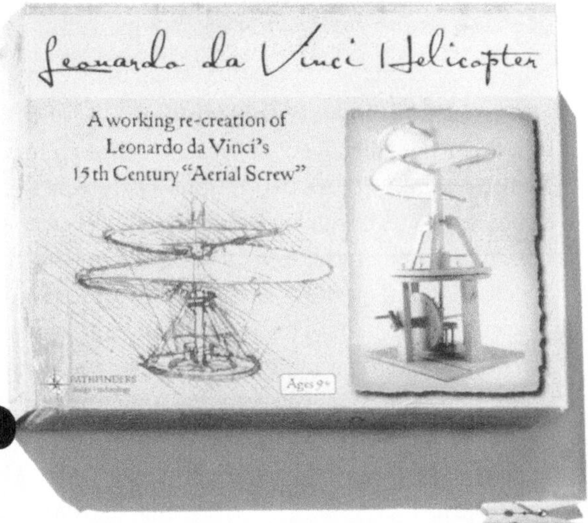

or

In a paradoxical turn, Leonardo was both a master of faithful representation and a heretic. Whereas his art remained respectful to nature, his designs sought to transcend it.

What is it to "invent" something? The Latin *invenio* can mean either "discover" or "invent," though in English we tend to think of these two actions as quite distinct. Discovery, sometimes, is barely an action at all, but simply a lucky circumstance; invention, by contrast, is thought to involve both an initial mental conception of something new and the execution of a plan to bring that thing into existence. According to this rather demanding conception of invention, it must be admitted that Leonardo was not nearly as prolific an inventor as is often believed. He did not "invent" a mechanical flight suit, a helicopter, a diving apparatus, a scythed battle chariot, a self-propelled vehicle, or a machine gun, so much as imagine a form their possibility might one day take.

It is also worth asking what sort of things may be invented. On the narrowest definition, inventions are contraptions, machines, or artificial devices that one can maneuver and manipulate. In Leonardo's era, inquirers were increasingly coming to see natural bodies as machines created by God. In 1543, Andreas Vesalius published his monumental work *De humani corporis fabrica*. The title translates roughly as "On the Structure of the Human Body," but the key term, *fabrica,* is in fact very difficult to translate. In both current Italian and French it means "factory," and suggests something more like a complicated system of pipes and vessels, of intake and output of energy; in a word, a machine. Leonardo as well, some decades earlier, saw his own anatomical studies as involving "geometrical demonstration . . . and calculating the forces and strengths of the muscles." This was then part of the same endeavor that guided him in his study of the human body, and for this reason it is admittedly forced to treat Leonardo The

Inventor separately from Leonardo The Scientist or Leonardo The Artist. He was simply busy *conceiving machines*: some natural, some artificial. Some of these conceptions made their way to paper, some made their way into three-dimensional and functional models, and some, no doubt, remained in his mind, and so were fated to die, in 1519, along with the natural machine of Leonardo's own mortal body.

Leonardo spent many years trying to master the artistic depiction of both flowing and swirling water. The great art historian E. H. Gombrich suggests that the artist was effectively trying to offer a "visualization of forces," trying to represent, that is, how natural dynamic systems function in general. In the mid-17th century the French philosopher René Descartes proposed his own so-called "vortex theory," according to which it is cosmic "vortices," or whirlpools, that are the basis for the formation of all organized bodies, from the solar system to the bodies of animals.

From Wish Lists to Dreams Come True

Historians of science have begun to appreciate that far more important than the actual appearance of a new invention is a desire that such an invention should exist. Thus, compilations of *desiderata*, wish lists, are studied to find out what people in past centuries were striving to bring about. And once an item appears on a list, it is nearly certain that it will eventually appear in reality. In the 17th century, alchemists began dreaming of "flexible glass," and some centuries later there was plastic. They dreamt of great fireballs that would sit in towers outside of the great cities, and provide those

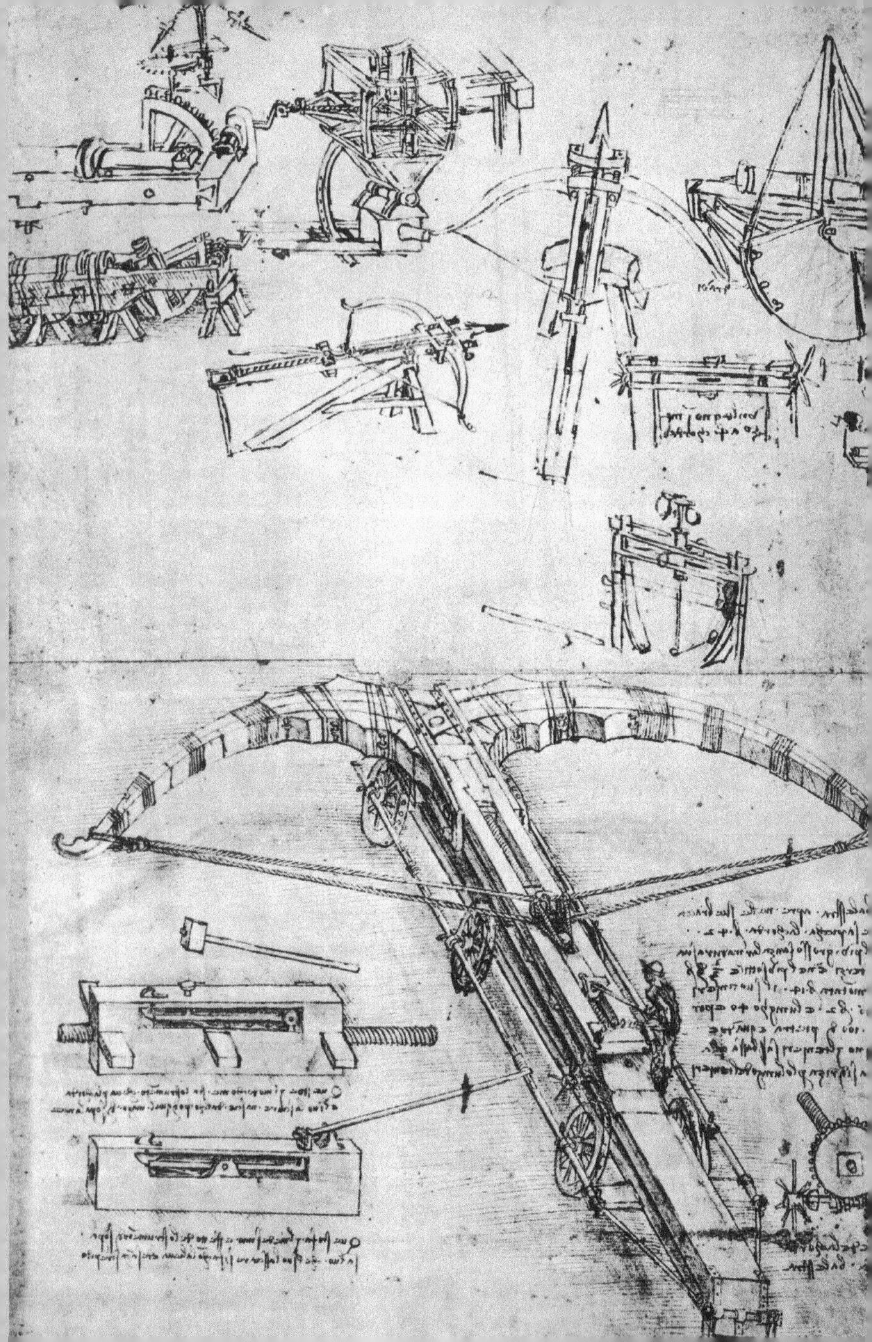

cities with constant heat and light. Eventually, for better or worse, we got our nuclear power plants.

At the end of the 15th century, machines were still principally driven by weights, springs, coils, and gears. Hydraulics and pneumatics were also in use, as well as "cyborg" technologies combining the power of living animals with that of moving vehicles. But the paradigmatic machines from antiquity through the Renaissance were ones that required no outside fuel, but were driven simply by the physical force of their interworking parts: mechanics. All the schools of invention were largely determined by what had already come before them; it was a rigid profession guided by century-old ideas.

Creative, visionary, and otherwise peaceful people were absorbed into the system of perpetual preparation for war.

During Leonardo da Vinci's time, the boundaries of what could be constructed by human ingenuity seemed suddenly to shift. As he and a few of his contemporaries came to understand, the best way to determine whether a machine could be built was not if the ancients had already spoken of it but, simply, to build it. This realization was, no doubt, aided by crucial innovations appearing in East Asia and the Islamic world, which

Leonardo offered his skills to war-waging rulers, as seen in his sketches of a "ballista," *a giant crossbow, circa 1500.*

The humble ball bearing is so crucial to modern technology that in World War II Allied bombers would often prioritize attacks on German ball bearing factories over munitions sites. There is some evidence that they had been conceived for the first time in the Roman Empire, and they would not be officially patented and manufactured until the late 18th century. But Leonardo's sketches of ball bearings from 1498–1500 give the first evidence of understanding how they would work.

gradually filtered into the European consciousness: the magnetic compass, the spherical astrolabe, the geared clock, explosives. Since the ancients had failed to realize, and in some cases even to conceive of, such technologies, it's not difficult to imagine Leonardo asking, "Why should we not, then, also be able to realize our own imagined machines?"

These broad considerations are preliminary to, and necessary for, placing Leonardo's contributions to the history of technology in proper perspective and context. In spite of a recent historiography that trends toward minimizing or deconstructing his actual accomplishments, he was the quintessential inventor: a composer of wish lists, a sketcher of possibilities.

Leonardo's Résumé

What we know of Leonardo's work as an inventor is derived mostly from his "notebooks," which are, in fact, pieces of paper that were widely scattered among Leonardo's friends and eventually collected into a handful of major codices: the *Codex Arundel* at the British Library, the *Codex Atlanticus* at the Biblioteca Ambrosiana of Milan, and the *Codex Leicester*, which now belongs to software mogul Bill Gates.

Most of Leonardo's drawings of machines were completed between 1478 and his earlier days in Milan, around 1482. From the beginning, his interest in mechanics and engineering was deployed in the service of political powers. In his introductory letter to Ludovico Sforza, the Duke of Milan, written between 1482–83, in anticipation of his arrival in the duke's service, Leonardo boasts:

> *Having now sufficiently seen and considered the experiments of all those who consider themselves masters and makers of instruments of war, and seeing that the invention and operation of said instruments differ in no way from those in common use, I am emboldened, without prejudice, to make myself known to Your Excellency, revealing my secrets.*

Then he lists his various abilities as an engineer, which are considerable and lengthy and touch on everything from portable bridges to mobile artillery. It comes as something of a relief when Leonardo eventually arrives at talents that are useful "in peacetime," mentioning "the construction of both public and private buildings, and channelling water from one place to another." Though a single text, the letter plainly reveals the intricate connection between patronage, politics, and large-scale technological projects. Then, as now, war, or the threat of it, was the principal motor of innovation. Creative, visionary, and otherwise peaceful people were absorbed into the system of perpetual preparation for war, the *Quattrocento*'s own military-industrial complex.

A Harmony of Three Parts

Throughout the letter to Sforza, Leonardo is intensely focused on water as a natural property: how it moves, how it can be crossed, or diverted, or withheld. He does not seem to be interested in harnessing its power as a source of energy for his machines. Similarly, with air, he is not interested in pneumatics, but in aerodynamics; to put air to use by understanding it. Nowhere is this clearer than in his designs for an "ornithopter," which is to say a machine that enables human beings to fly inside a contraption that simulates the flight of a bird. Here again we come across the difficulty of separating his work as an inventor from his work as a scientist. In order to realize the ornithopter he first had to discover the secrets of avian flight. This is no simple problem of aerodynamics, but rather the result of millions of years of subtle adaptation in the structure of the bodies of birds. In the *Codex on the Flight of Birds*, likely written around 1505–07, he draws a clear line from the study of the properties of air, to the physiology of birds and the aerodynamics of their flight, and, finally, to the possibility of moving from understanding these things to the mechanical flight of

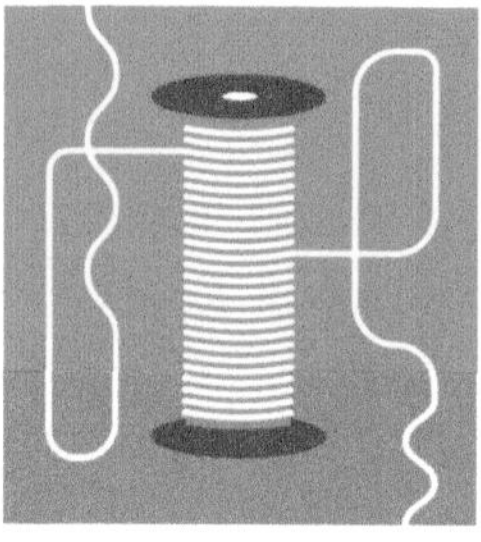

Art and science. Many of the engineering projects and inventions Leonardo was working on also found their way into his paintings. In the *Madonna of the Yarnwinder*, the baby Jesus is holding a device that would prove very important: one of Leonardo's few undisputed successes as an inventor was to devise a plan for constructing automated bobbins for winding great lengths of thread.

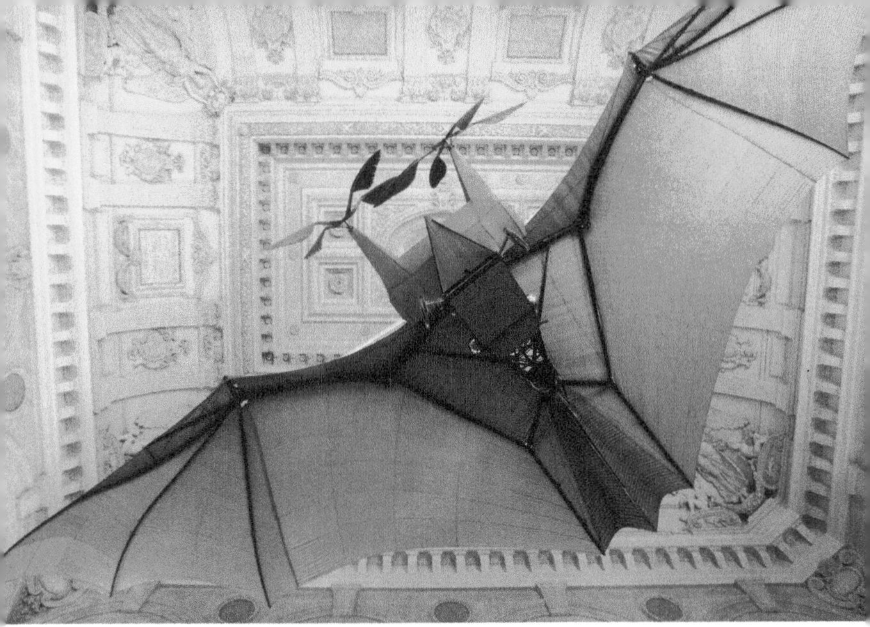

French engineer Clément Ader, whose steam-powered Plane 3 *failed to take flight in 1897, also based his designs on bird anatomy.*

human beings. Thus, in a series of sketches that appear to depict birds in different forms of flight, Leonardo notes "when the bird is in the air without beating its wings in a position of equilibrium without the benefit of the wind, it means that the geometric center and the center of gravity correspond." Yet on the following page of the *Codex*, remarkably, he switches from a third-person description of the bird, to a second-person address to an unidentified "you": "If the wing and the belly are too far above the wind, then you must lower the opposite wing to allow the wind to strike and push upward, thus righting yourself." The illustration next to this text appears to be the very same bird as before. But might it also be a birdman for Leonardo, if only potentially?

Here, as elsewhere, Leonardo's greatest aim in his inventions is, so to speak, to ride with nature, not to fight against it or to force it to do what it is not intrinsically disposed to do. He is determined to understand what nature does—as in the flight of birds—and use what it already does in order to thrust human beings into situations where they do not naturally belong, but rather to enable them to realize their innate potential. Birds fly by nature, and human beings inquire. The final result of this inquiry is that humans, too, by nature, will fly.

In the *Codex Atlanticus* Leonardo offers an observation that places his ornithopter project within the broader context of his philosophy of nature and of technology. He writes:

> *A bird is an instrument working according to mathematical law. It lies within the power of man to make this instrument in all its motions, but without the full scope of its powers; but this limitation only applies with respect to balancing itself. Accordingly, we may say that such an instrument fabricated by man lacks nothing but the soul of man.*

Here he aligns himself with a fairly common understanding of natural beings, such as birds, which extends back to Aristotle, and which holds that they have their own sort of "soul." In this conception, the soul does not confer immortality or the possibility of salvation, but rather functions only as the principle of activity in the creature—the source of vitality and striving that enables the body to carry out its functions, and, thus, to be distinguished from a mere corpse. A machine that a human being might build to simulate the flight of a bird cannot possibly, no matter how elaborately the parts are constructed, be imbued with an avian soul. So, the science of mechanics must learn to reproduce what nature does, but without the vital principles. This is what distinguishes our "artificial machines" from "natural machines." Ours must be built, while those of nature are generated, and then grow from unknown vital principles, from seeds or germs or bare potentialities spread throughout all of nature. A machine that must be built is in the end only an imitation of a natural being, and, for the most part, what it is able to do is a faint shadow of the capacities of the creature that inspired it.

But look: who is that climbing into the ornithopter, or dreaming of climbing into it? The history of technology is also the history of prosthetics: human beings constructing, or imagining machines that will extend the capacities of their own ensouled bodies. And when this occurs, the human-machine hybrid may come to have "the full scope of powers" of the things of nature that human ingenuity has sought to imitate. The human soul, or "consciousness," as we prefer to call it these days, has the power to project itself out into the world. Human beings are, so to speak, the external souls of the machines they invent. And this, perhaps, is why we have such a sharp sense of coming to know Leonardo's own soul when we study his machines; some were only dreams, some he managed to conjure in real life, and some would only be materialized centuries after his death. The history of technology is as much a history of conceiving and drafting as it is a history of building and executing. Simply to come up with a machine in one's mind is already, in a certain sense, to invent it. The rest is filling out the details.

Ahead of His Time

VISIONARY INVENTIONS

Leonardo's designs for machines are often said to have anticipated or foreshadowed inventions that would later become familiar features of the modern world. But how do his designs really compare to their modern descendants?

Leonardo's Invention	Modern Interpretation
1. Ornithopter	Airplane
2. Golden Horn Bridge, Turkey	Vebjørn Sand Bridge, Norway
3. Diving apparatus	Scuba gear
4. Aerial screw	Helicopter

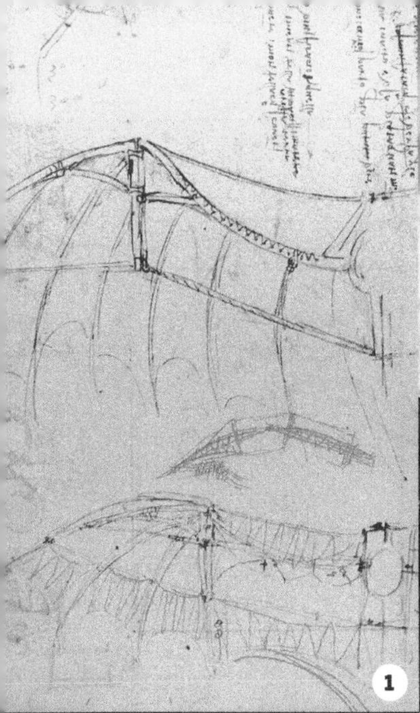

1

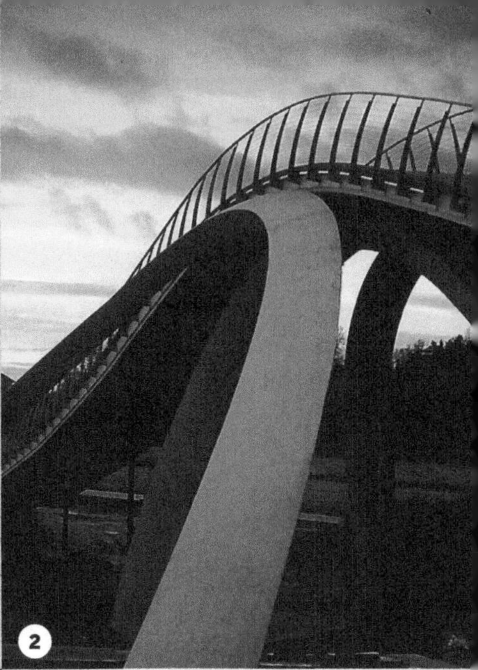

2

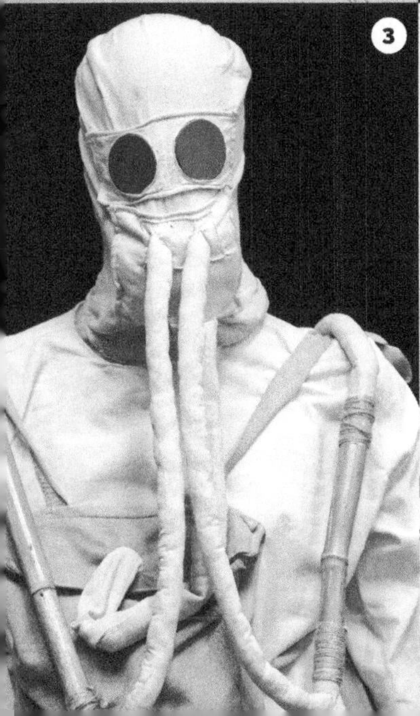

3

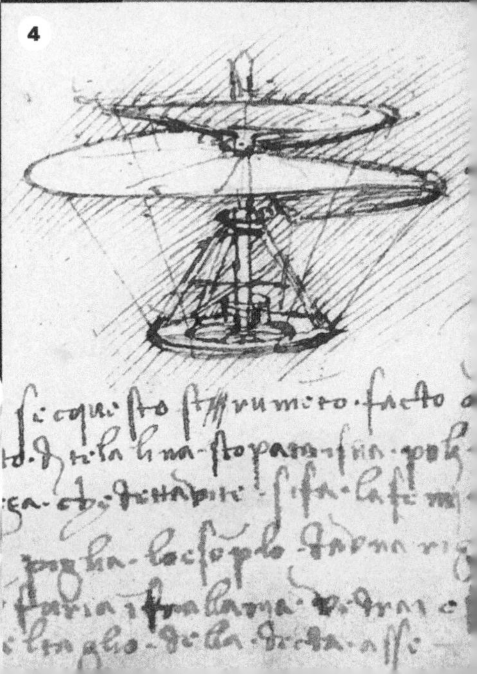

4

REPORT No. 5522

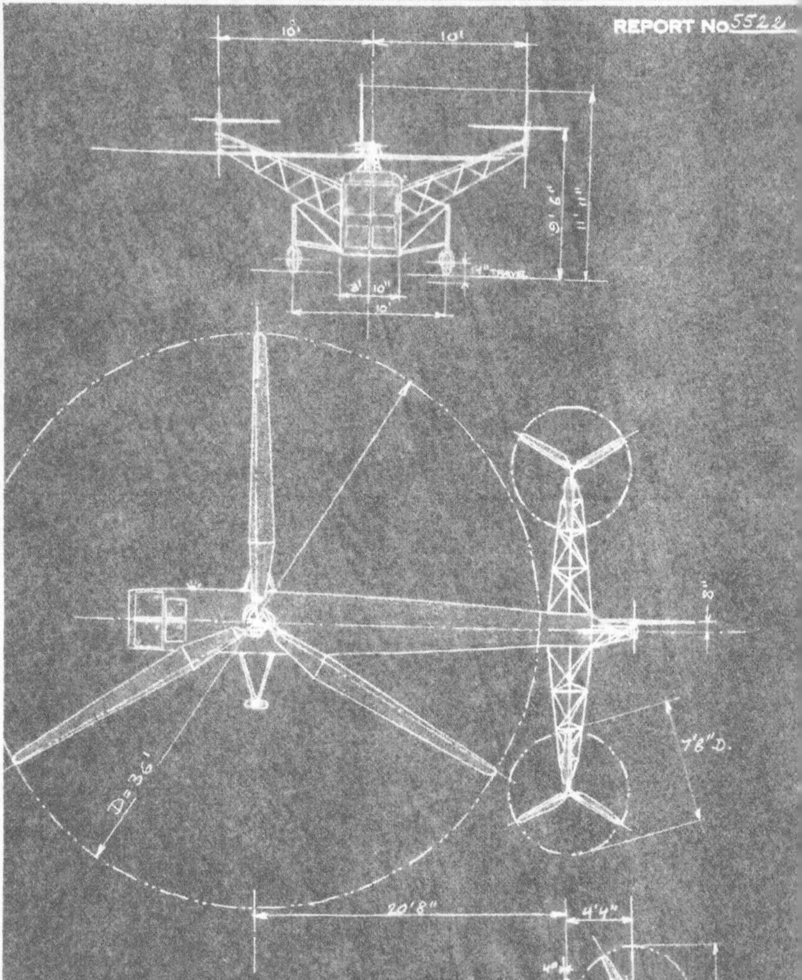

The Wonder of Flight

Leonardo and the vexing laws of gravity

Why can't humans fly? Honestly, it seems as if there was something overlooked during Creation, a capacity we feel we naturally ought to have, and yet one that we can only realize with significant artifice and ingenuity. We even dream we can fly, as if recalling in sleep some primordial ability we've lost. The myth of Icarus warns us not to carry this dream into waking life, telling us it's hubristic to set about making it a reality.

Reliable reports of aviation experiments—using kites, lanterns, bamboo copters, and balloons—began to appear in China in the first millennium BC. The Andalusian polymath Abbas ibn Firnas jumped off a tower in a glider around 850, and in the following centuries we know of several attempts at flight in gliders and other winged devices. Some of these attempts were fatal, and no doubt there were many other

Igor Sikorsky, the engineer who first patented a helicopter design in 1932, had been inspired since childhood by Leonardo's ornithopter sketches.

deaths in the early history of flight that went unrecorded. With each fatality, the warning issued in the myth of Icarus resounded among the survivors.

A Wasted Dream?

Leonardo da Vinci does not seem to have taken humanity's inability to fly as anything more than a temporary circumstance. Yet it is in his designs for human aviation that Leonardo is often criticized for allowing his fancy to carry him away. Already in the biographical account given by Giorgio Vasari in 1550, we find the expression of regret that he wasted so much energy on devising flying machines, energy that could have been spent creating still more immortal works of art. In the 19th century the great French poet Paul Valéry described Leonardo's dreams of flight as an expression of utopian excess. "When he dreams of building a flying man," Valéry writes, "he sees him take off to seek snow on the peaks of the mountains, and return to scatter it over the town streets shimmering in the summer heat." The poet is, in a way, right. All dreams seem impossible when they are first uttered; even what now seems as mundane as air conditioning was once an impossibility.

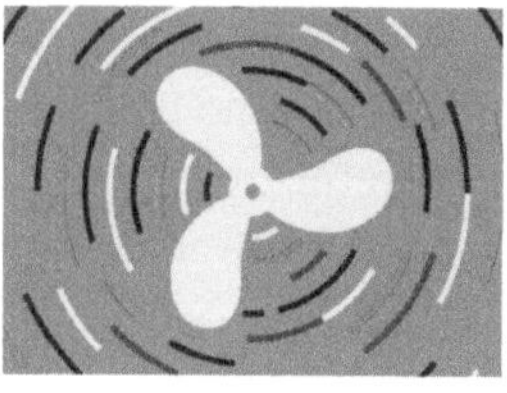

Even if Leonardo's aerial screw had not been too heavy to lift off of the ground, it would have quickly spun out of control once in the air. As early designers of functional helicopters would come to understand, they also need sideways thrust from a rotor in order to fly.

Leonardo engaged intensely with the problems of flight from roughly 1478 on. His earliest designs of wings for humans seem to have been produced on the occasion of a passion play, presumably for the costume of an angel, and thus were likely not intended to facilitate actual flight, no matter their anatomical correctness.

In the early months of his first stay in Milan, around 1485, he began to seriously think about how to achieve human flight. His great innovation was one that relied on his ingenious skills as a scientific observer and as a draftsman. He gradually came to understand that if progress is going to be made in artificial flight, it can only be done by understanding natural flight, and by depicting its mechanical principles with unprecedented exactitude. Drawings from that time, now included in the *Codex Atlanticus*, show several different models for possible flight machines, some of which have the man within standing upright, and others showing him lying parallel to the ground, like a bird. The sketches from the early 1490s, now found in the *Codex Madrid*, are notably more sophisticated,

Did You Know

Leonardo based many of his sketches for theoretical flying contraptions on the example he had readily available: the anatomy of birds. Most birds have a keel, or carina, that extends from their sternum and provides them with leverage for flight. Obviously, human bodies have no such thing, and are in fact entirely unfit for flight. Yet birds have served as the most useful model from nature for the creation of flying machines usable by human beings.

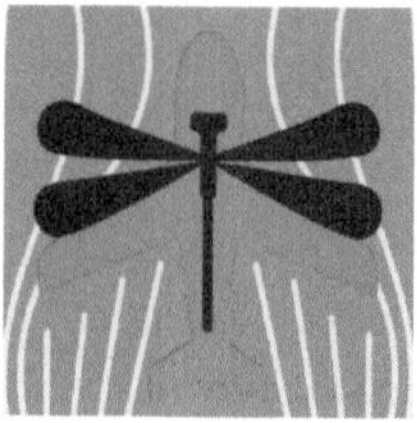

Leonardo studied dragonflies as well as birds when designing his ornithopter. These would have provided a model of flight that is particularly difficult to reproduce, since most species are outfitted with forewings that can beat out of sync with the rear wings, giving them a high degree of lift with very little thrust.

and, according to some scholars, give evidence of concrete attempts to construct working models of the devices drawn and to test them in reality. There is no sign, however, of either success or failure. We at least know that Leonardo himself survived this period, so if a flight apparatus was tested and crashed, he was probably not in it.

Sometime between 1503 and 1506, Leonardo employed a significantly new approach in comparison to earlier designs. As Edoardo Villata has sharply observed, Leonardo's terminology shifts from the "instrumental" to the "zoomorphic": from now on, the future possibility of human flight will develop out of the present reality of avian flight. But if the "instrumental" approach is rejected in favor of the one that looks directly to nature, this is only because "the bird is an instrument that operates according to mathematical law." Perhaps, then, we might revise Villata's account to say that Leonardo does not so much shift from an instrumental to a zoomorphic approach, but instead he comes to recognize that zoomorphs, provided by nature, are the paradigm and model for what human-made instruments might be.

Former British rugby player and Royal Air Force pilot Rory Underwood tests a 1989 flying machine based on Leonardo's 15th-century design.

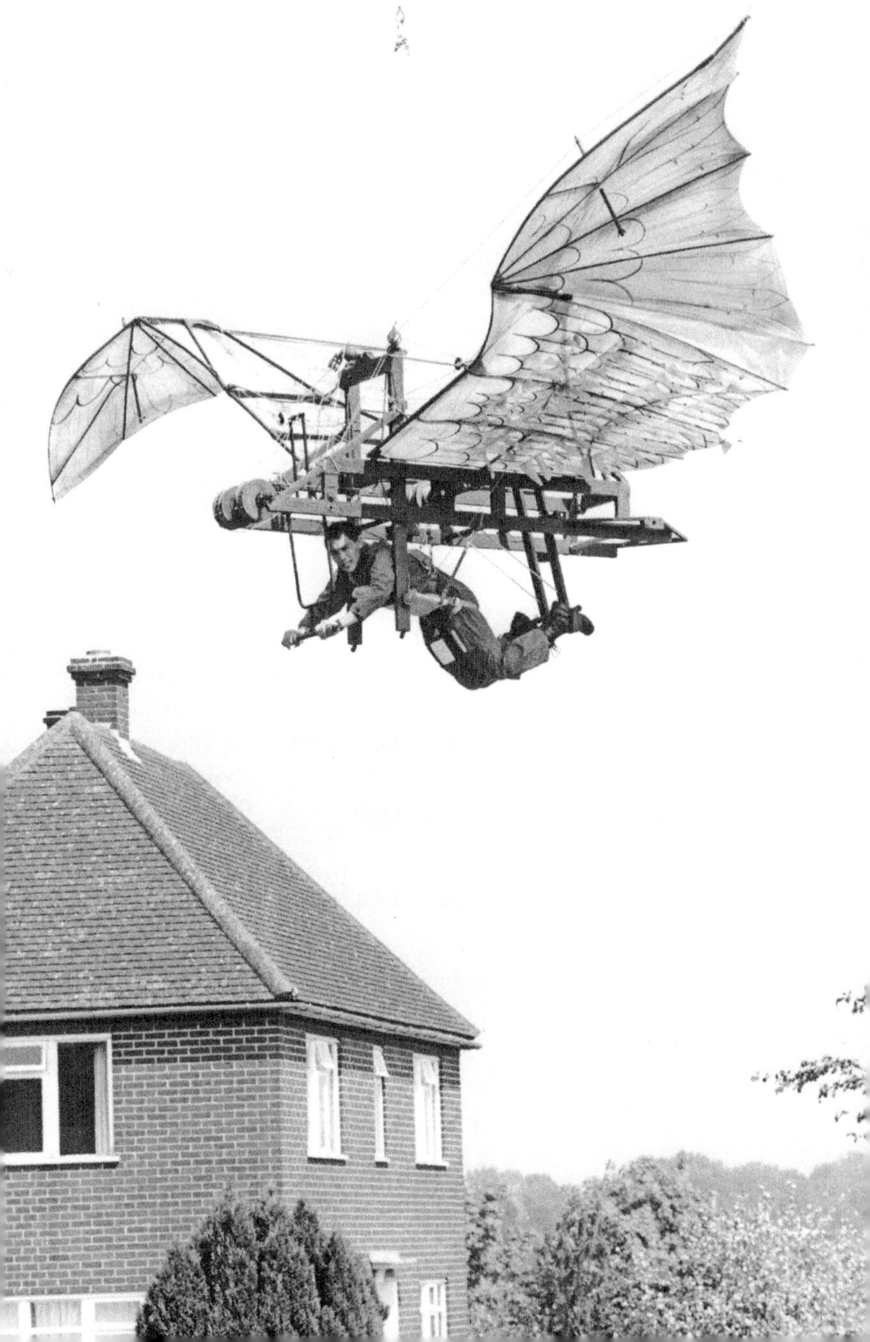

Did You Know

Throughout the late 19th century several unmanned rubber-band-driven ornithopters were successfully flown by a number of French inventors. The German aviation pioneer Otto Lilienthal, who had studied with particular attention the physiology of the flight of storks, began to design an ornithopter in 1894. His plans for it were cut short when he died in a glider accident (also of his own design) two years later. Just before dying in a Berlin hospital with a fractured spinal column, he uttered his final words: "Sacrifices must be made."

It is around this same period that Leonardo wrote the *Codex on the Flight of Birds*. Whereas in earlier designs he had been preoccupied by the problem of how to generate enough force to flap wings fast enough to lift a human being, now, having truly watched the birds, he was struck by how little flapping many of them actually do. They are not all designed on the model of the hummingbird; some, such as the kite, "do not flap their wings very much, but seek the current of the wind." The kite does not work against nature, but rather moves with it. This, the author seems to understand, is the model to follow, not the frantic hummingbird, whose physiology is a wonder of nature but not the best model to be followed by human beings.

A 16th-Century Helicopter

Not all of Leonardo's designs for flight were inspired by birds, of course. His designs for an "aerial screw," a sort of helicopter in the shape of a top that would move directly upward simply by pushing air downward in its rotation, were first drafted in 1493. Commentators have often stressed the novelty of this design, some even identifying it as the first model for a heavier-than-air craft that would lift off from the ground.

There may have been a physical model constructed of Leonardo's aerial screw. It is generally agreed that if it was tested, given what we know of the materials that were likely involved, it would have been far too heavy to fly. But here, as elsewhere, the question of success or failure in the inventor's own lifetime is not so important. We have helicopters now, after all.

Helicopters did not, of course, simply appear from a single attempt to transform a blueprint into a prototype. There were slow approximations and failures in physical reality to realize what was, soundly or unsoundly, first conceived on paper or in computer models.

Today it is expected that the bulk of labor involved in producing aircraft will occur in the design phase, and, once the design is right, physical realization is really only the final stage of the process. Leonardo's work stands at a pivotal point in history. Although he likely never brought about working flight machines, it may be that his real "inventions" were the designs themselves—signalling a turn toward increasing abstraction in the history of technology, a change which in the following centuries would become the greatest factor in the rapid surge of technological innovation.

And yet, while Leonardo da Vinci moved toward abstraction, he at the same time grounded innovation in attention to what is most concrete, what has always been there, inviting us to pay attention to it. According to him, nature, which gives us birds and maple seed pods, holds the blueprints of everything we might ever hope to accomplish.

Draining the Swamps

FUTURIST AND CIVIL ENGINEER

One of Leonardo's enduring preoccupations, alongside flight, was the drainage and canalization of large bodies of water. Water would also prove to be one of the most difficult challenges in his work as a draftsman: how to draw it, how to capture its qualities in two dimensions. As early as his letter to the Duke of Milan, he boasted of his extensive knowledge of hydraulic engineering, and was particularly keen on using this knowledge for military applications. Some decades later, in 1514, he would be sent by Giuliano de' Medici to drain the Pontine Marshes in the area around the city of Terracina in the Lazio region of central Italy. These marshes had been responsible for frequent outbreaks of malaria in Rome, and since antiquity they had vexed geographers, statesmen, and generals alike in their liminal suspension between land and water.

The Greek geographer Strabo had noted that those wishing to cross the marsh could only do so in a boat pulled by a donkey. Barely had Leonardo arrived to begin the project when he contracted malaria. As far as is known, he had never suffered from a serious illness before. He was already in his 60s, and he presumed that his end was near. He began to prepare his friends

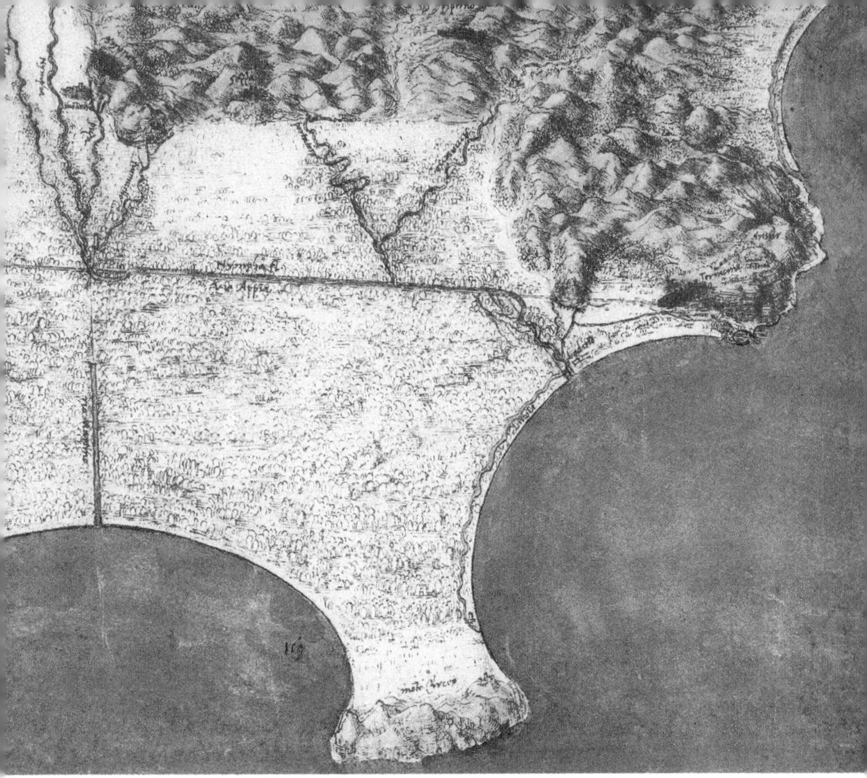

Leonardo's drawings of the Pontine Marshes were part of the Duke of Milan's plans to drain and "reclaim" them, something not realized until the 1930s under order of Benito Mussolini.

for his departure, and making arrangements for the bequeathing of his belongings. Following this infection he in fact lived another five years, but as someone who sharply felt his own mortality for the first time, he knew he only had a limited amount of time left and had to use it wisely. Soon he would enter the service of the king of France, and depart for that country in 1516. In the last three years of his life, he was principally engaged in courtly ceremonies and pomp, and did not, in fact, drain any swamps.

The Scient

Leonardo's contributions to the birth of modern science were enormous. But did *he* think of himself as a scientist?

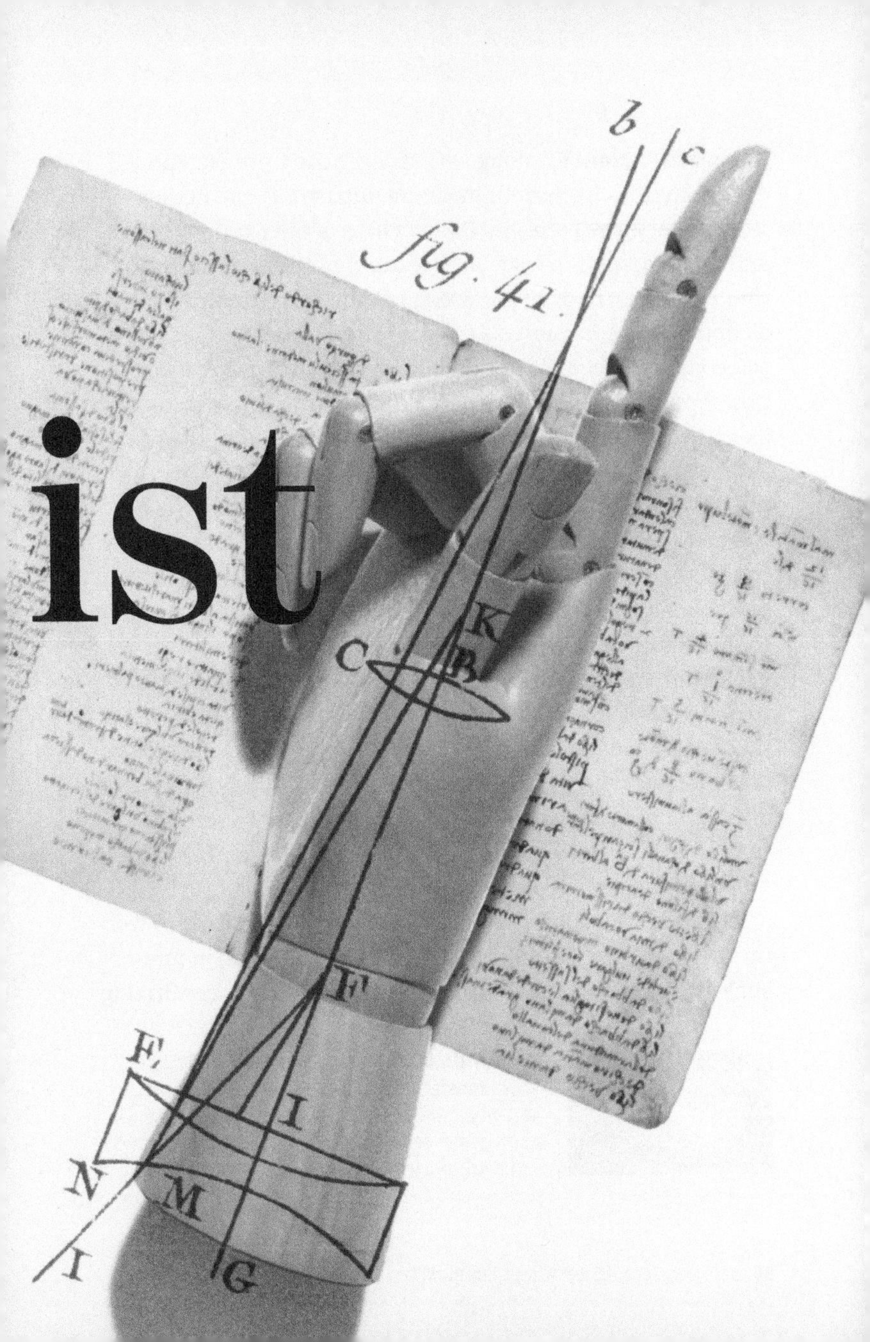
ist
fig. 41.
b
c
K
C
B
F
F
I
N
M
I
G

The word "science," along with its agentive form "scientist," did not take on its current meaning until sometime in the 19th century. The Latin and Italian forms of the word, *scientia* and *scienza*, were in frequent use during the Renaissance, but they denoted a body of knowledge of any sort. Theology, for example, was considered a science, since it was a cohesive and self-contained set of doctrines, however much of it was speculation about the non-empirical realm. What we today think of as natural science was in turn conceived in the Renaissance as "natural philosophy." In fact, the "natural" part of this phrase was often implied, and "philosophy," understood as the investigation of the natural world, was often juxtaposed to theology as "worldly wisdom," meaning knowledge of the mundane in contrast with knowledge of the divine. According to these archaic usages, we may say that Leonardo was a consummate philosopher, in that he was constantly seeking to understand the workings of nature. He was not much of a theologian, at least not in the strict sense. Yet he believed, as many Renaissance thinkers did, that all of nature is a sort of unfolding of divine wisdom, that divine wisdom somehow translates into natural order, and that the study of this order must, therefore, reveal the greatness of God.

This is not how the authorities of Church and State received the discoveries of the natural philosophers. While an inquirer such as Leonardo might have thought of his work as confirming

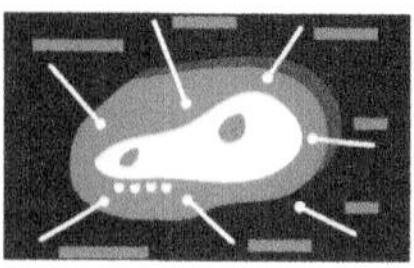

Leonardo is the first to have identified ichnofossils as the traces of animal activity in the distant past. But many of his contemporaries were unprepared to recognize even ordinary fossils as the traces of animals.

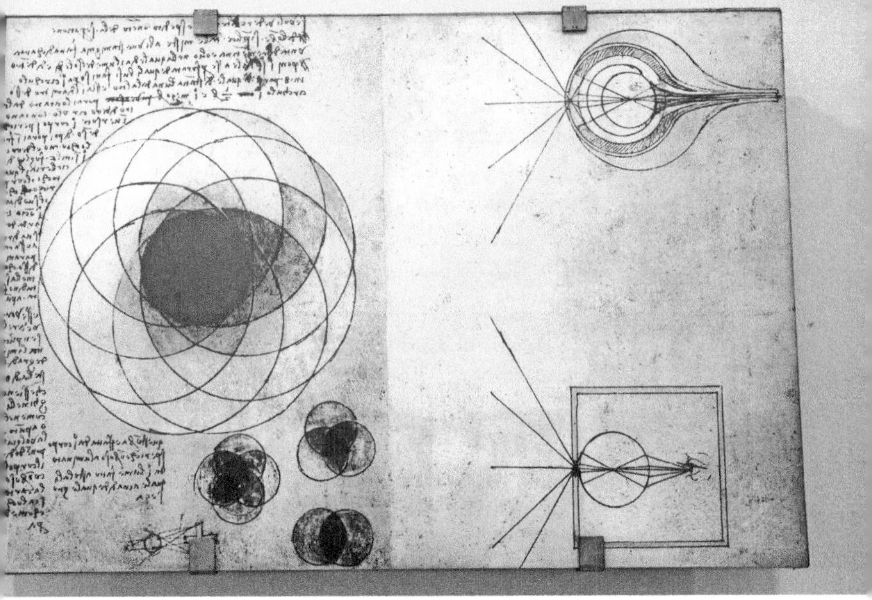

The Codex Atlanticus, *a 1,119-page collection of Leonardo's drawings and musings, includes this 1490 depiction of the eye's functioning.*

and buttressing piety and reverence for the divine, those in power were more likely to see it as merely complicating matters, as probing where we naturally have no right to look, or, in the worst case, as turning up facts that appear to be in direct contradiction with revealed truth.

The old Aristotelian Catholic philosophers supposed that "to know" is to have mastered a received doctrine, passed down by authorities from one generation to the next. A 17th-century Aristotelian did not need to look through a telescope to learn whether the sun has spots or not, since Aristotle (who of course did not have access to a telescope) already had said many centuries earlier that the sun is composed of a homogeneous substance throughout. Leonardo, by contrast, considered the senses to be the most reliable source of knowledge, and when they contradict what Aristotle taught, then so much the worse for the Greek philosopher.

In the Renaissance it was precisely this attitude that defined a "philosopher." Thus, in his 1550 biography, Giorgio Vasari writes of Leonardo: "And so many were his caprices, that, philosophizing of natural things, he set himself to seek out the properties of herbs, going on even to observe the motions of the heavens, the path of the moon, and the courses of the sun." Vasari imagines here a sort of spiralling out, from the microcosmic order of nature here on Earth, toward the heavens, the macrocosm, eventually understanding the entire order as a unified whole. The tone is somewhat mocking; he takes Leonardo's philosophical side as a detriment to the further perfection of his artistic ability. To "philosophize," on Vasari's understanding, which was typical of the era, was to dabble in inconsequential things, or even worse, to be drawn in by the satanic temptation of making nature's power your own.

According to Giorgio Vasari, Pope Leo X is said to have been very enthusiastic about "philosophy," by which he meant natural science. In 1513, Leonardo was invited to stay at the Vatican in order, partly, to study the technology of burning mirrors and to promote science. This seems to have pleased the pope for a while, yet the following year Leonardo was denounced by his own associates to the Roman pontiff for having, evidently, probed too deeply into the secrets of nature.

A Rare Combination

The line between Leonardo da Vinci's art and science is seldom clear, and this is perhaps nowhere more muddied than in the study of human anatomy. His anatomical investigations were important principally for the new standard of exactitude they set in anatomical illustration, rather than for the discovery of any hitherto unknown organs or systems. He also sincerely believed that the proportions of the human body could be understood geometrically, and that, when they were, he could also understand the way in which the human being embodied the basic principles underlying the natural world.

In his earliest anatomical work, circa 1489–90, Leonardo was interested in representing the human body in its ideal aspect, as with *The Vitruvian Man*, rather than in its complicated reality, as seen in a bisected couple engaged in intercourse. His knowledge, however, was influenced by earlier masters of the field, and in the coition drawing we can see the transmission of false beliefs, such as a sperm duct connecting the penis to the spinal column, based on an ancient idea that the male semen is a rarefied product of cerebrospinal fluid. He depicts what he imagines—on the basis of the authority of tradition—must be there, rather than verifying for himself.

When he returns to anatomical study around 1508–10, his approach will be radically altered: empirical, rigorous, exact. In 1510, he traveled to Pavia to study anatomy with Marc Antonio della Torre whom Vasari, in keeping with the usage of the day, describes as "an excellent philosopher." In a remarkable passage from around this period, Leonardo describes the immense

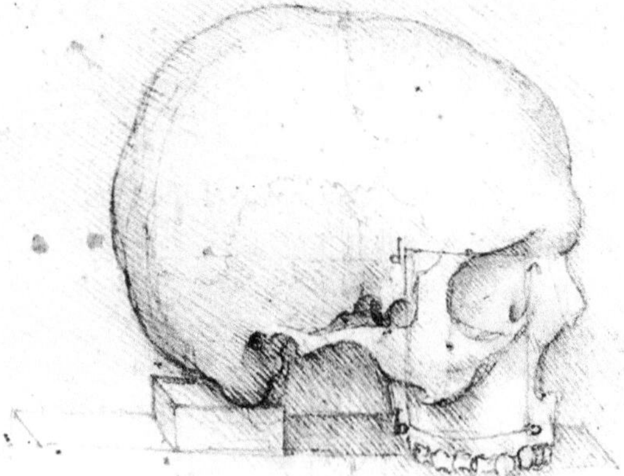

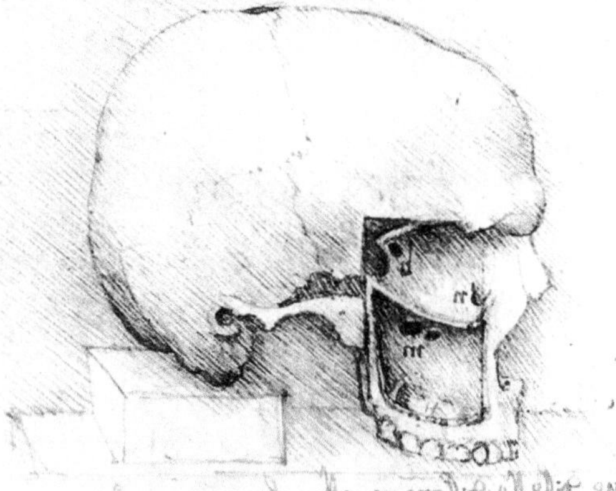

Leonardo's anatomical drawings, like this detailed sketch of a skull, show how little distinction he saw between science and art.

strain and difficulty of anatomical research, while also revealing his own understanding of its alliance with art:

> *Though you may have a love for such things you will perhaps be impeded by your stomach; and if this does not impede you, you will perhaps be impeded by the fear of living through the night hours in the company of quartered and flayed corpses, fearful to behold. And if this does not impede you, perhaps you will lack the good draughtsmanship which such a depiction requires; and even if you have skill in drawing, it may not be accompanied by a knowledge of perspective; and if it were so accompanied, you may lack the methods of geometrical demonstration and of calculating the forces and strengths of the muscles; or perhaps you will lack patience so that you will not be diligent."*

His eventual point is that he himself possesses this rare combination of abilities. And, yet, he would not have been in a position to actualize them had the circumstances not allowed it, specifically if he hadn't had access to cadavers. The practice of human dissection remained highly controversial in the early 16th century. In the Renaissance, these taboos began to collapse, but the procuring of human bodies remained tightly controlled. Many great anatomists are known to have engaged in illegal grave robbing, although studies were mostly conducted in close collaboration with legal authorities; the bodies often came directly from the gallows to the dissecting table. It helped for an anatomist to be well connected to judges and magistrates, as Leonardo was.

Reading the Book of Nature

If a human being embodies the geometrical principles on which all of nature is built, then the study of anatomy is already itself a window, perhaps a telescope, looking out onto the rest of the world. Leonardo was capable of taking a wide focus as well, reflecting on cosmology and on the motions of the heavens in a number of notes. There is even some evidence that he anticipated the Copernican heliocentric model of the universe. In a context-free comment jotted on what art historian Martin Kemp has identified as one of Leonardo's "scrappiest and untidiest" manuscripts, he observes: *El sol non si move*, "The sun does not move." In truth the author could have meant any number of different things by this, and nowhere does he provide us with a sustained account of the order and motion of the celestial bodies in the solar system.

Copernicus and Darwin represent two great heresies: one removing the Earth from its special place in the cosmos, the other removing humanity from its special place in the history of life on Earth. Leonardo partially anticipated both of them. While he did not speculate about a possible evolutionary past, he did speculate about a prehistory of the Earth that could not be made compatible with the biblical account of origins. In particular, he defended a version of what would later be called "uniformitarianism," the idea that the same processes that brought about the formation of the Earth and its features (continents, mountains, oceans, and so on) are still going on right now and can be discerned in ordinary geological phenomena. This view contrasted with "catastrophism," according to which the basic features of the Earth are static and came into existence in a relatively short period of time as a result of major events—such as the biblical flood. In his years serving the Duke of Milan, Leonardo was interested in accounting for the seashells in the mountains around the Lombardy region. He concluded that it would not be enough to suppose that they were sent there in one great wave during the flood since, in fact, different geological strata contained different varieties and quantities of shell. He inferred from this that at different times the area that is now Northern Italy must have been underwater and, indeed, that areas currently underwater could eventually protrude. The amount of time needed to account for such changes was vastly longer, as he seems to have understood, than biblical chronology could permit. But Leonardo could not deny the evidence of the senses.

Another significant contribution to paleontology was Leonardo's identification of traces: the fossilized remains of the burrows, tunnels, and other signs of the activity of ancient animals, now known as ichnofossils. He identified these clues as potentially valuable sources of information in reconstructing

The printing press appeared in Europe toward the tail end of the 15th century, at just the moment Leonardo was reaching the peak of his career. At the same time, book metaphors proliferated. While such images certainly pre-dated the era of the printed book, suddenly in the 16th century descriptions of nature as being itself a "book" abounded. Today we often ask whether physical reality is a "hologram," or whether the mind is a "computer." Might it be that these supposedly profound questions are really just a reflection of the present state of human technology?

More than 100 years after Leonardo's death, the great Danish naturalist Nicolaus Steno would settle in Florence, under the patronage of the Medici family, in order to research anatomy and paleontology. Like his Italian predecessor, he believed that human anatomy is underlain by geometrical principles and, also, that seashells and fossils testify to the slow, uniform development of the features of the earth's surface. Unlike Leonardo, in 1667 Steno converted to an austere version of Catholicism that required him to abandon his interest in scientific inquiry.

the Earth's past. The Earth's surface, he understood, is abounding in signs ready to tell the story of how things came to be the way they are.

A common Renaissance trope was the idea of the "Book of Nature:" that God created the world in the expectation that human beings would eventually learn how to read it and discover the secrets of Creation. This trope persists in Leonardo da Vinci's work, but the idea of a particular author of this "book" is heavily subdued. It is not that God "wrote" the ichnofossils into the ground with a particular intention that we would decipher them, but they are there, now, and we can decipher them with our own ingenuity. In this, God is subtly replaced by nature itself as the source of our knowledge. In his anatomical research Leonardo speaks of "the first composer of such a machine" as the human body, by which he means God. As Martin Clayton and Ronald Philo have observed, he usually prefers to speak simply of *l'opere mirabile della natura*, "the marvelous works of nature." Nature writes her own book, so to speak, and this is what the new "science," of which Leonardo is harbinger and prophet, is concerned with learning to read.

do the math

48.8cm: ***Width of a 1502 aerial-view map of the Val di Chiana drawn by Leonardo. Val di Chiana itself is around 100 km wide, which means that the features on the map are .00000488 the size of the real-life features to which they correspond.***

49 square meters: The proposed area for a parachute, designed in 1485. In 2000, a skydiver in South Africa made a landing using a parachute constructed to Leonardo's specifications.

6000: The number of rounds per minute fired by the M134 Minigun machine gun, the highest rate of any service weapon. In addition to a machine gun that would run on a tread-wheel, Leonardo designed a multi-barreled gun, consisting in 3 rows of 11 guns fastened together on a single revolving platform. The earliest functional machine gun, the Gatling gun, first released in 1862, was able by 1876 to fire as many as 1200 rounds per minute.

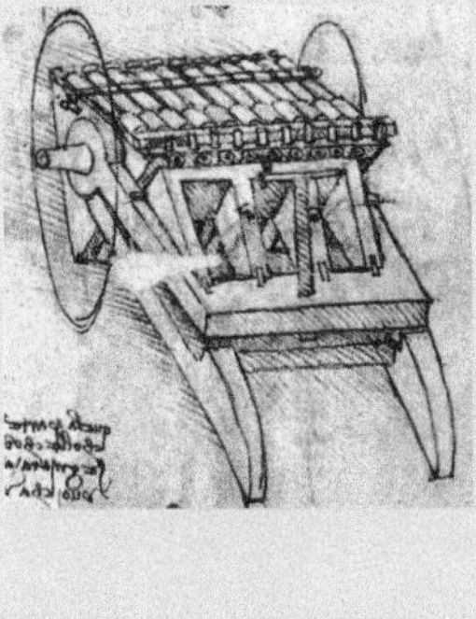

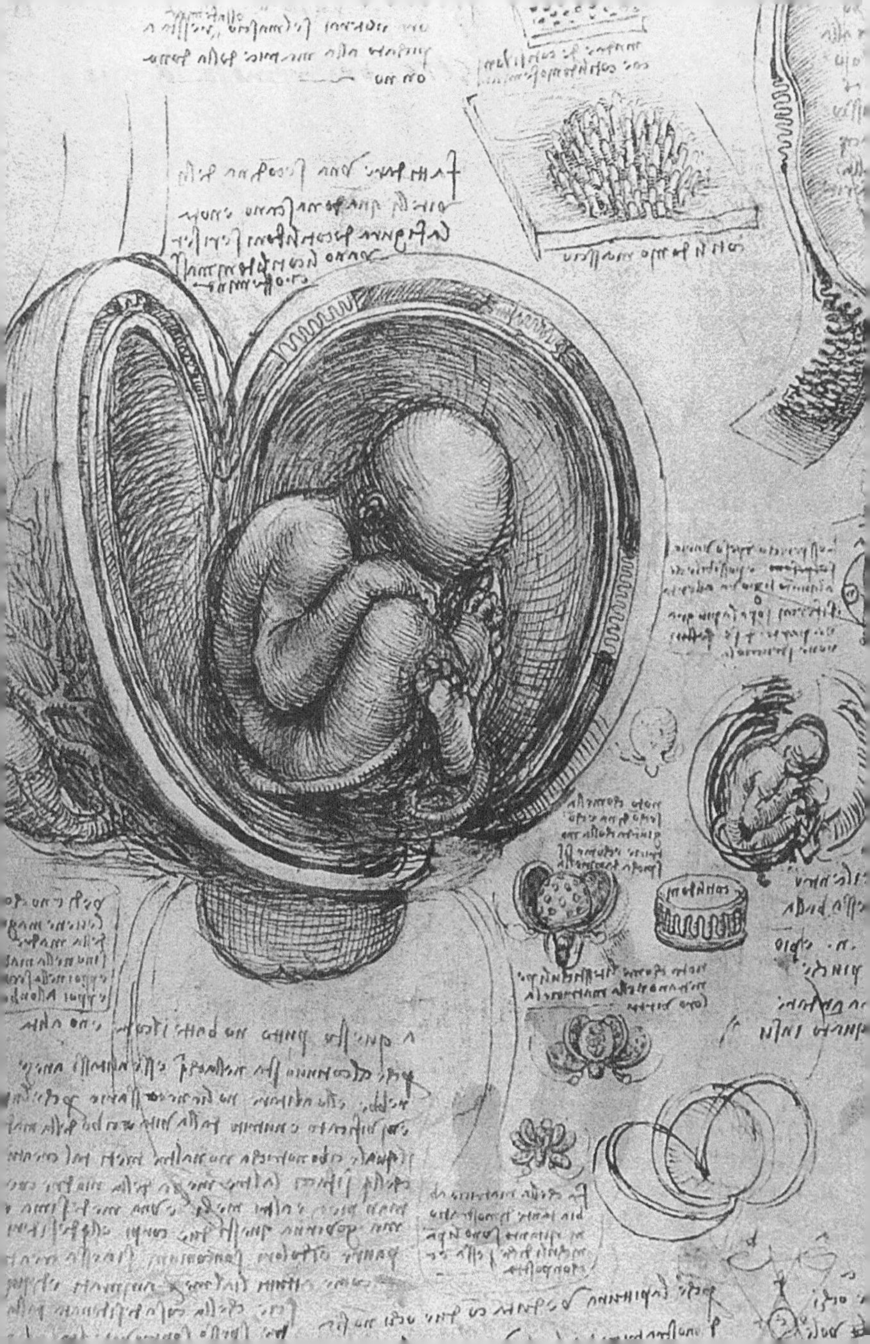

The Anatomy of a Birth

Much of what we know today about the womb can be traced back to Leonardo

Leonardo da Vinci's embryological studies of 1510–12 show him at the height of his skill as an anatomist. He is the first-known researcher in history to cut open a pregnant human cadaver and describe what he saw. Perhaps no other domain of knowledge had been considered more secret, and more off-limits, than the development of the fetus in the womb.

A long tradition of lore surrounded the process of fetal development: that the child is imbued with a soul on the 40th day; that in the eighth month, but not the seventh, premature birth is highly dangerous; that several different men can contribute sperm to the generation of a single child in a process known as "superfetation" (today, the term refers to a pregnancy that occurs when the mother is already pregnant).

The precision with which Leonardo observed anatomy, as in this rendering of a fetus, gave name to the robotic "da Vinci Surgical System" used by doctors today.

Fetuses were sometimes seen following a miscarriage, but they were quickly swept away in shame and secrecy. It was not until the 17th century that systematic study of fetal development in other mammals would be carried out, when William Harvey carefully slaughtered several doe at different intervals after having observed them in copulation. Around the same time, René Descartes attempted his speculative fable of the process of embryogenesis as a blind mechanical series of motions of particles. We can get a human being, the French philosopher argued, or at least a fully functioning human body, simply by heating up clots of blood.

Shared Souls

Leonardo had no revolutionary theory of fetal development. It is almost certain that he retained a broadly Aristotelian conception of the process, in which development is guided along by an immaterial principle that moves the unformed mass of matter from which the fetus grows toward some fixed goal or end, in the same way that a blueprint "guides" the motions that eventually bring about the construction of a house. This immaterial principle is a soul, or something similar to it. Recourse to such an entity seems today like a failure to remain true to the scientific evidence, but in the absence of a science of genetics such an immaterial principle seemed rather a necessary hypothetical entity, without which no sense could be made of how such a complex, organized being as a human emerges from the mixture of simple fluids. Although his remarks are, as usual, very succinct, Leonardo appears to break with tradition by arguing that the fetus shares its soul with the mother until birth. His reasoning for this conclusion is that the fetus cannot breathe while in the womb, since it is surrounded by water, and that it cannot eat either, in the usual sense, since its food comes through the umbilical cord attached directly to the mother's body. Thus, nutrition and respiration—two bodily functions that classically were seen as governed by the soul—are absent for the duration of gestation. Moreover, Leonardo adheres to the common belief that changes in the mother's emotional state, particularly sudden frights or intense desires, can be communicated to the fetus and imprinted in its developing body. "A thing desired by the mother is often found imprinted on those parts of the infant that have the same qualities in the mother at the time of her desire; and a sudden terror kills both mother and child." From this Leonardo concludes: "Therefore . . . the same soul governs and nourishes in both bodies." It is likely that the soul Leonardo imagines to be shared between mother and fetus is only the "sensitive" and "vegetative" soul, that is, the parts of the classical tripartite human soul responsible for

Did You Know

In Leonardo da Vinci's most famous drawing of a fetus in the womb, he depicts his subject in a breech position, meaning that the baby's feet, instead of the head, are posed toward the birth canal. One of the smaller drawings on the same sheet, however, suggests that he believes the baby rotates in the womb at the time of birth for a normal, headfirst delivery.

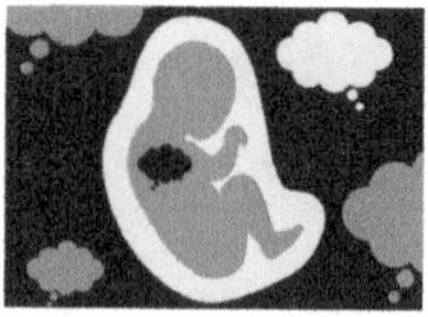

Many theorists in the history of embryology supposed that the mother's thoughts, often influenced by what she saw, could be communicated to the developing fetus and consequently seared into it in the form of birthmarks.

normal bodily function and growth. This would not prevent him from supposing, in accordance with tradition, that at some point during gestation the soul, which is entirely non-bodily and immortal, is injected into the fetal body by God, or by some other non-biological occurrence.

The placenta that Leonardo da Vinci includes in his drawings of a human fetus is evidently borrowed from his observations of bovine placenta (he had recently dissected a cow). Thus, like Galen and other ancient sources of medical knowledge, he too is prone to infer, sometimes incorrectly, from animal physiology rather than from direct observation. As scholars Martin Clayton and Ronald Philo suggest, it is likely that in the pregnant cadaver Leonardo dissected, the discoidal placenta was damaged or no longer visible, and so he simply replaced it with the cotyledonous placenta familiar from cows. Even the most thorough observers make substitutions and inferences. Why he never attended a human birth to study a human placenta is lost to history. One common question in the history of embryology concerned the degree of similarity between animal and plant reproduction. Leonardo perceives a high degree of similarity, and even maintains that "all seeds have an umbilical cord which is broken when the seed is ripe."

Leonardo not only studied the fetus, but also carefully observed and described female reproductive anatomy. His sketches reveal a concern to understand the way female anatomy, including the muscles surrounding the pubis, is arranged to facilitate childbirth. Leonardo broke more than one taboo here: not only was he mingling with the dead, he was also probing into that vital process that had long been held a carefully guarded secret of nature. What he saw, in human anatomy as everywhere else, was nature's wisdom. He wrote, for example, of how "nature has provided" for the elimination of the fetus's urine "by making a channel in the fundus of the bladder through which urine goes from the bladder to the umbilicus and from the umbilical cord to the mouth of the uterus." As he cuts through taboos, there is no shame or regret, only wonder, and confirmation of his belief in nature's power to shape its productions in the best possible way.

We know that Leonardo was not unfamiliar with the feeling of terror dead bodies can induce, and we may suppose that he also knew the feeling of pity and sorrow at the sight of a prematurely deceased woman and her dead fetus. But Leonardo da Vinci does not seem to have worried about what others might have seen as "desecration." For him, scientific inquiry cancelled out what might have been desecration, and indeed turned the cutting and the probing into a sort of redemption. Leonardo embodies the spirit of the late Renaissance, which had only just begun to look at the dissection of bodies in a way that was no longer warped by taboo and fear. In this new spirit, death might still be a misfortune, but the best we mortal beings can do to mitigate this evil, to some extent, is to confront it straight. We can probe into its most ghastly products, the corpses of our fellow humans, and attempt to figure out how it exercises its horrible power.

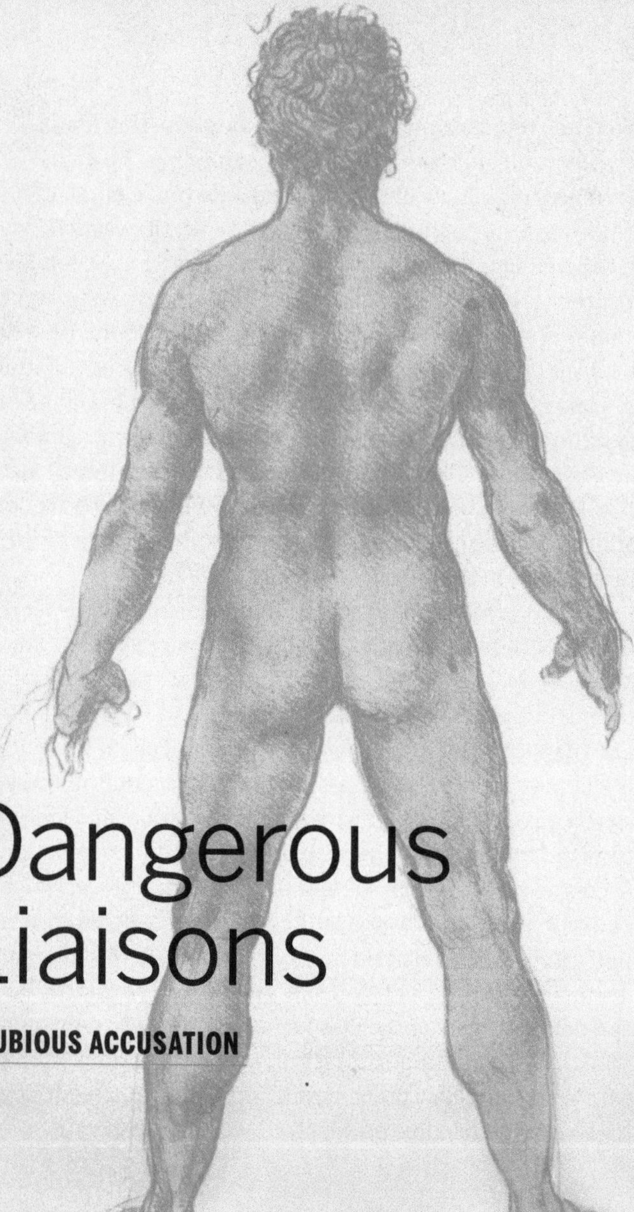

Dangerous Liaisons

A DUBIOUS ACCUSATION

In 1476, Leonardo was anonymously denounced, along with several other prominent young Florentines, for homosexual liaisons with the male prostitute Jacopo Saltarelli. The charges were eventually dropped, most likely because one of the accused was a close relation of the powerful Medicis. Saltarelli himself may have been a model for painters, and the "sodomy" in question may have been any number of things, including simple debauchery. It may also not have been as scandalous as we imagine. In Leonardo's era, "Florentine" was often a euphemism for "homosexual," and there was a surprisingly high degree of acceptance of same-sex relationships among the elite. This may in part have had to do with the revival of Platonic ideals of love, which took love between men to be the most exalted human relationship, and physical love between them as a sort of step on the way toward pure "intellectual eros." There is no sign of Leonardo for the following two years, but in 1478 he turned up in the service of the Medicis, with the most prestigious and sought-after patronage a young artist could hope to acquire. Scholars throughout the centuries have described Leonardo as "chaste," but there is significant evidence that after the Saltarelli case he would have at least two more significant relationships. In Gian Paolo Lomazzo's 1563 fiction, *Il libro dei sogni*, the character representing Leonardo is asked whether he had "played the game from behind which the Florentines love so much." Leonardo replies: "And how many times!" The real Leonardo himself left behind a pornographic sketch representing this very game, played with his protégé Salaì. The evidence is clear enough. What seems more in need of explanation is the scholarly hesitation to acknowledge it.

Leonardo's lost fresco, Battle of Anghiari, *was based on several anatomical studies, such as this chalk drawing dated circa 1504.*

A Man of All Things

The paragon of human potential

The term "Renaissance man" (as well as less gender-specific variants) has passed into our way of speaking to denote a person who is learned in a wide array of subjects. The phrase contrasts with "specialist," and is held to embody everything that our current system of education and professional training discourages. In some respects, it is true that science as currently practiced allows little room for the Renaissance man. Science today is a massively collaborative endeavor, and the best way for it to advance is for each participant to play a very circumscribed role, taking responsibility for a tiny sliver of the entire, vast project. This system works well, yet often produces scientists who have a range of knowledge that makes them much more like technicians than intellectuals in the proper sense.

The 1490 Vitruvian Man *is exemplary of both the artist's fascination with proportions, and his view that the body is a microcosm of the universe.*

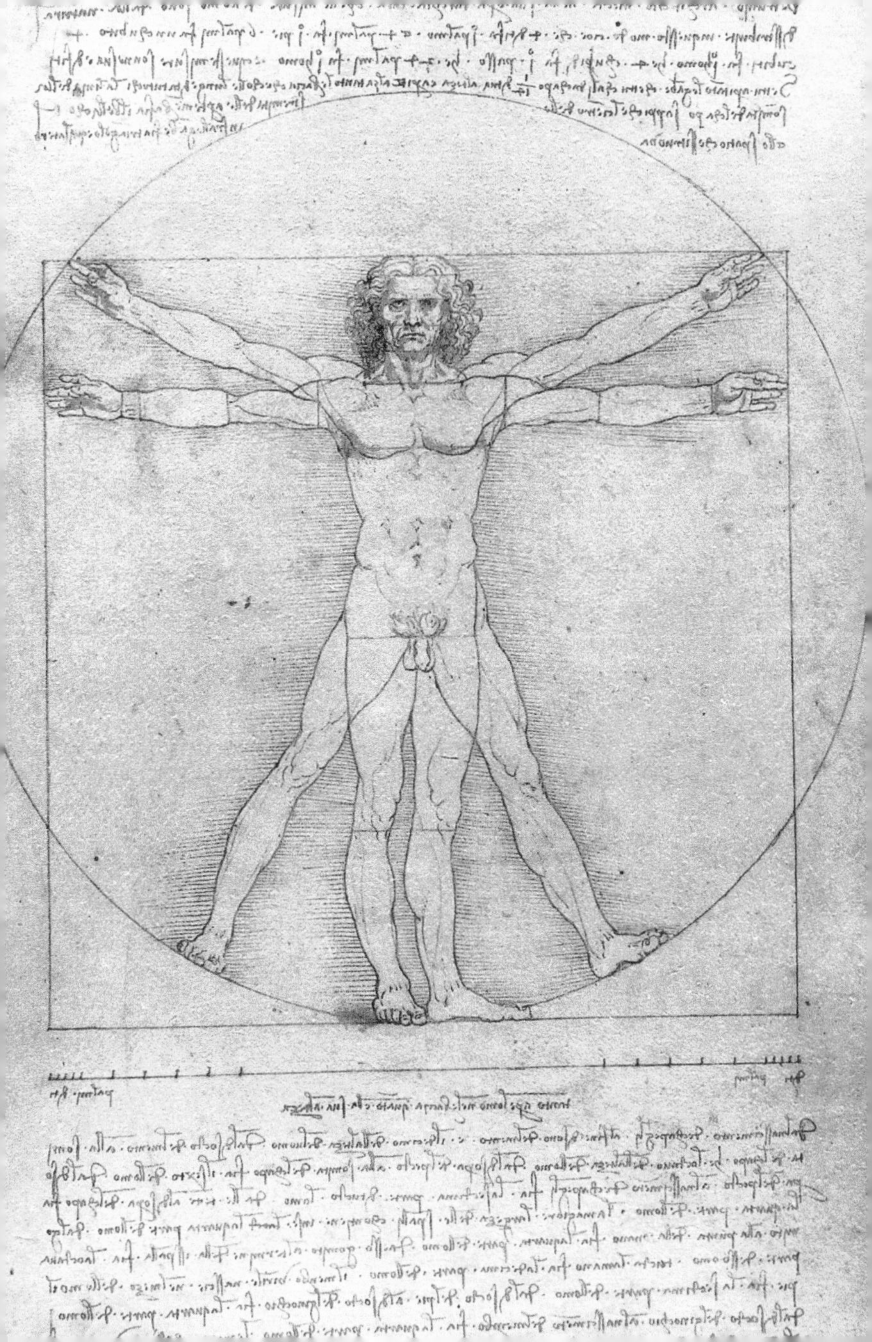

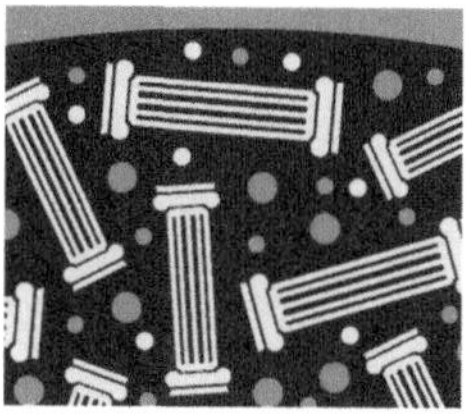

One of the crucial factors in the shift from the medieval to the Renaissance periods was the fortuitous discovery of the stunning monuments, columns, and statues that had been built in ancient Rome and had gradually been buried under the earth. Little by little, a sense emerged among late-medieval Italians: we, too, could achieve such splendor.

Typical of this division of labor is the mistaken presumption that a scientist will have no competence in the arts and humanities. This is the famous "two cultures" problem diagnosed by C. P. Snow in the 1950s. The idea began to emerge in the 19th century, but was completely unknown in the Renaissance and early modern eras. At that time, "science," though it did not yet exist under this name, was a preeminently human endeavor, and to come to know the natural world was inseparable from the Renaissance humanist project of realizing the full extent of human potential.

Was Leonardo a Renaissance man? He is often cited as the paradigmatic example of this type, and indeed he made tremendous contributions in many areas. Yet he was principally a practitioner, a maker, a doer. He was not particularly interested in theorizing about matters that afforded him no opportunity for intervention, direct observation, or building and creating. His theoretical understanding of how the world works, of mathematics and the laws of natural motion in particular, was surely much greater than what he reveals in his writings, since he had to master these domains in order to carry out the practical projects we know he did.

In part, his range of abilities was a direct reflection of the expectations that would ordinarily be placed on a courtier seeking patronage. As Baldassare Castiglione writes in his influential *Il Cortegiano* (the courtier), a gentleman who "lives at the court of princes" must seek out "the ability and knowledge perfectly to serve them in every reasonable thing, winning from them favor, and praise from other men." Leonardo surely loved to pursue knowledge for its own sake. It is no less certain that he loved the favor and praise lavished on him as a result.

Though he was an artist, this area of activity was not conceived or undertaken on the presumption of a distinction between art and science. Today in universities, we speak of "arts and sciences," and we understand that the former include the humanities while the latter exclude both fine arts and what in continental Europe are still called "the human social sciences": economics, psychology, sociology, etc. But, for Leonardo, fine art existed on a continuum with the natural sciences, and draftsmanship was for him an essential component of the investigation of nature, while in turn he was not particularly interested in the human sciences. He does not seem to have known Greek or to have excelled particularly in Latin or in the study of classical literature and poetry. If we think of the Renaissance in the literal sense as the period of rebirth of classical learning, then he is decidedly not a Renaissance man. He was not particularly impressed with the ancients, and would always prefer his own investigations over whatever the ancient authorities might have claimed about a given subject.

One of the key markers of the Renaissance was the rediscovery of classical Greek literature, but equally important was the gradual shift away from Latin to the contemporary “vernacular” or “vulgar” languages of Europe, such as Italian, French, German, and others. A key figure in this shift was the Italian author Dante Alighieri, a fellow Florentine, who in the early 14th century wrote the *Divine Comedy* in the vernacular Italian language. This work would help make it possible for Leonardo to write his own notes on his subjects of study in Italian, rather than being weighed down by Latin erudition.

Another important cultural transformation in the Italian Renaissance took place in the field of philosophy. Aristotelian philosophy had come to predominance in Western Europe with St. Thomas Aquinas in the 13th century, and would eventually harden into an institutionalized and rote system of learning often called Scholasticism. In this context, especially in the Italian Renaissance, Platonism was an important counter-current. The philosophy of Plato represented a somewhat dangerous potential for the rebirth of pagan values, including certain expressions of sexuality.

It might be most correct to say that Leonardo da Vinci was a scientific polymath. From his own point of view, his

?

Did You Know

Between 1346 and 1353, the population of Florence was cut roughly in half by the bubonic plague, also known as the Black Death. Some historians have argued that one result of this annihilation was the relative decline of elite power and a heightening of the power of commoners, which, over the long-term, resulted in the political and philosophical transformations we associate with the Renaissance: humanism, freedom, and the first steps toward egalitarianism.

range of interests likely seemed quite cohesive, even narrowly focused. He was intent on understanding, representing, and technologically duplicating the order of nature. In order to do this, he had to study mathematics, the various branches of mixed mathematics such as music and architecture, and the domains of nature in which mathematical order is realized, such as anatomy. He was not, by his own lights, spread too thin, though he does seem to have regretted late in life not having devoted more of his energy to the perfection of painting. This does not seem to be a regret at having wasted his life, but merely a regret about which there is nothing to be done: that there is not more time, or that we cannot lead several parallel lives.

The idea that Leonardo is the ultimate Renaissance man occludes from view the important fact that, in his era, the domains of knowledge were carved up differently, and affinities between them were perceived that have since been lost. In particular, there has been a radical transformation in society's expectations concerning the sort of things a scientist might reasonably be expected to care about. To put this point somewhat more bluntly, over the past few centuries the scope of science has been greatly reduced, impoverished, and increasingly distanced from other forms of engagement with the world around us. At the basis of this transformation is a change in our society's philosophical understanding of what nature is, and of what humanity's relationship to nature is. Science has become vastly more efficient, but its individual practitioners are more like ball bearings (of the sort that Leonardo himself designed) in a great machine than masters of the machine itself.

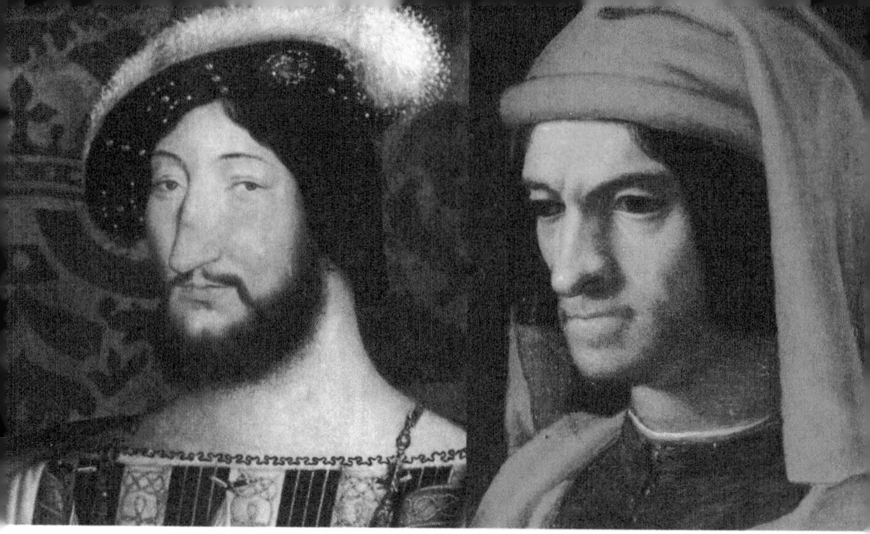

Enablers and Inconveniences

ARTISTS AND THEIR PATRONS

Over the course of his life, Leonardo created art and devised inventions and projects in the service of Lorenzo de' Medici, Ludovico Sforza, Cesare Borgia, Pope Leo X, King Francis I of France, and others. One might be tempted to disparage him as a "courtier," but, in truth, an aspiring Renaissance artist had no other choice but to enter the system of patronage. In this system, the artist was typically required to subordinate his own projects and sensibilities to the

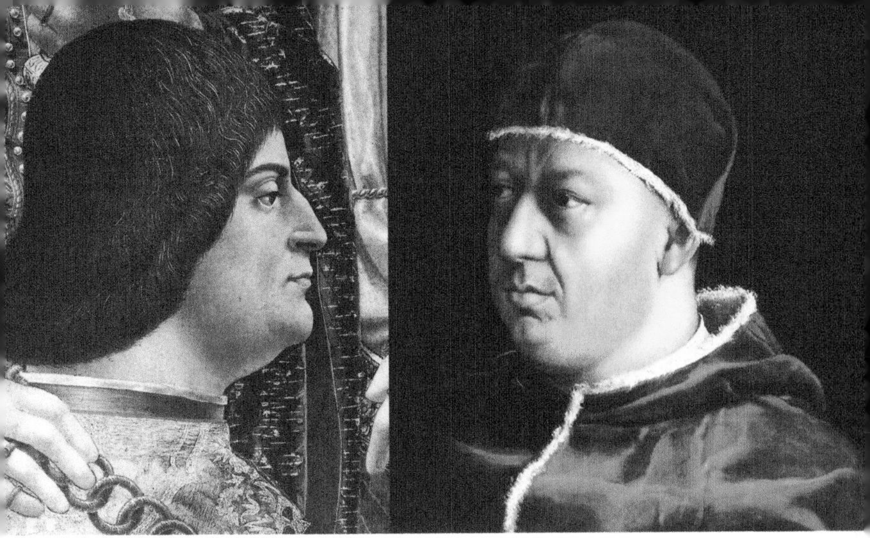

Portraits of aristocracy, from left to right: Francis I painted by Jean Clouet; Lorenzo de' Medici by Agnolo Bronzino; Ludovico Sforza by Master of the Palo Sforzesca; Pope Leo X by Raphael.

will of the aristocrat who paid him and, therefore, enabled him to do any work at all. As we see in Leonardo's letter to the Duke of Milan though, artists and artisans were sometimes very proud of the services they could provide, and their sense of their own identity and value was wrapped up in their ability to give a patron what he desired. Very often, the desired creations were machines for the improved waging of war. Then, as now, and as at any other moment of history, one of the important motors of innovation seems to have been the need, or perceived need, to keep enemies at bay, and to crush them with violence if necessary. Leonardo da Vinci himself was not bellicose, but he was perfectly willing to subordinate his genius and his imagination to the purposes of state—principally to weaponry and to military engineering but, also, secondarily, to pomp and ceremony—in exchange for the freedom to create.

COUNTERPOINT

Monolith or Man?

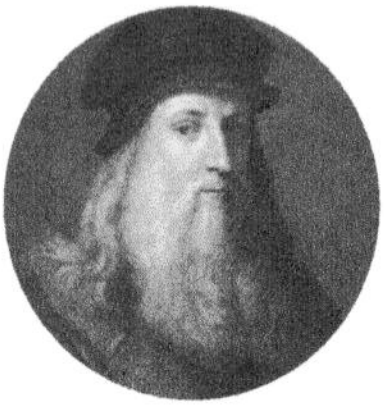

Was Leonardo's genius undermined by the broadness of his interests?

Leonardo was universally curious. He believed that evidence outweighed the wisdom of the ancients; that nature is undergirded by, and best understood through, mathematics; and that artistic representation of the world is a central part of exploring and understanding that world (in this respect, his work is governed by a vision of the unity of what we today call "art" and "science"). He was a genius, too; a genius artist and inventor, but not much of his story can be told by dwelling on this fact for too long. It is more revealing to focus on the reasons his genius was channelled in this direction rather than that, and to focus on his own understanding of the projects he sought to realize. It does him a disservice, in this regard, to dwell too long on his status as a "Renaissance man," where this means simply being interested in sundry things. Leonardo was not simply sniffing around wherever his nose picked up the faintest scent (to invoke the classical distinction between the fox—who was interested in many things but always superficially—and the hedgehog, who was interested in only one thing, but dug into it deeply). Leonardo evades this facile dichotomy. He was interested in everything, precisely because he recognized the unity of everything. He was also a human being: vain, ambitious, and sensuous. But "human," for Leonardo, was no insult. He did not seem to have worried about the spectre of sin that so many in his era saw, and so many today still see, lurking wherever and whenever a person looks too deeply into the secrets of nature, or follows his own desires too passionately. In this respect, he strikes us as human not in the sense of being flawed, though clearly he was, but in the sense that he so fully embodied the ideals of Renaissance humanism. He saw human beings as the greatest expression of perfection of the natural order (simultaneously downplaying the explicit role for a Creator of this order), and allowed his human flaws to imbue and enliven the productions of his genius. Some of his paintings are held to be false starts, even mistakes. Rigorous critics, such as Martin Kemp, have a very clear view of which of Leonardo's works are better, and which are worse, than others. Such judgments are based entirely on internal features of the works and, while perfectly sound and compelling, such critique belongs to a different sort of project than the one we are engaged in here: tracing the work back to the life and, in the knowledge that lives cannot themselves be judged, bracketing our critical faculties to the extent possible. Leonardo is often criticized for passing too quickly from one thing to the next, and for designing machines that could not possibly work. But he had considerable ground to cover, not because he was a restless, hasty, and curious fox, but because all these different projects were, for him, expressions of the same basic will. The order of nature is a unity, but it is also immense. And it was the nature of his genius, and of his humanity, to want to absorb it all.

PARTING THOUGHT

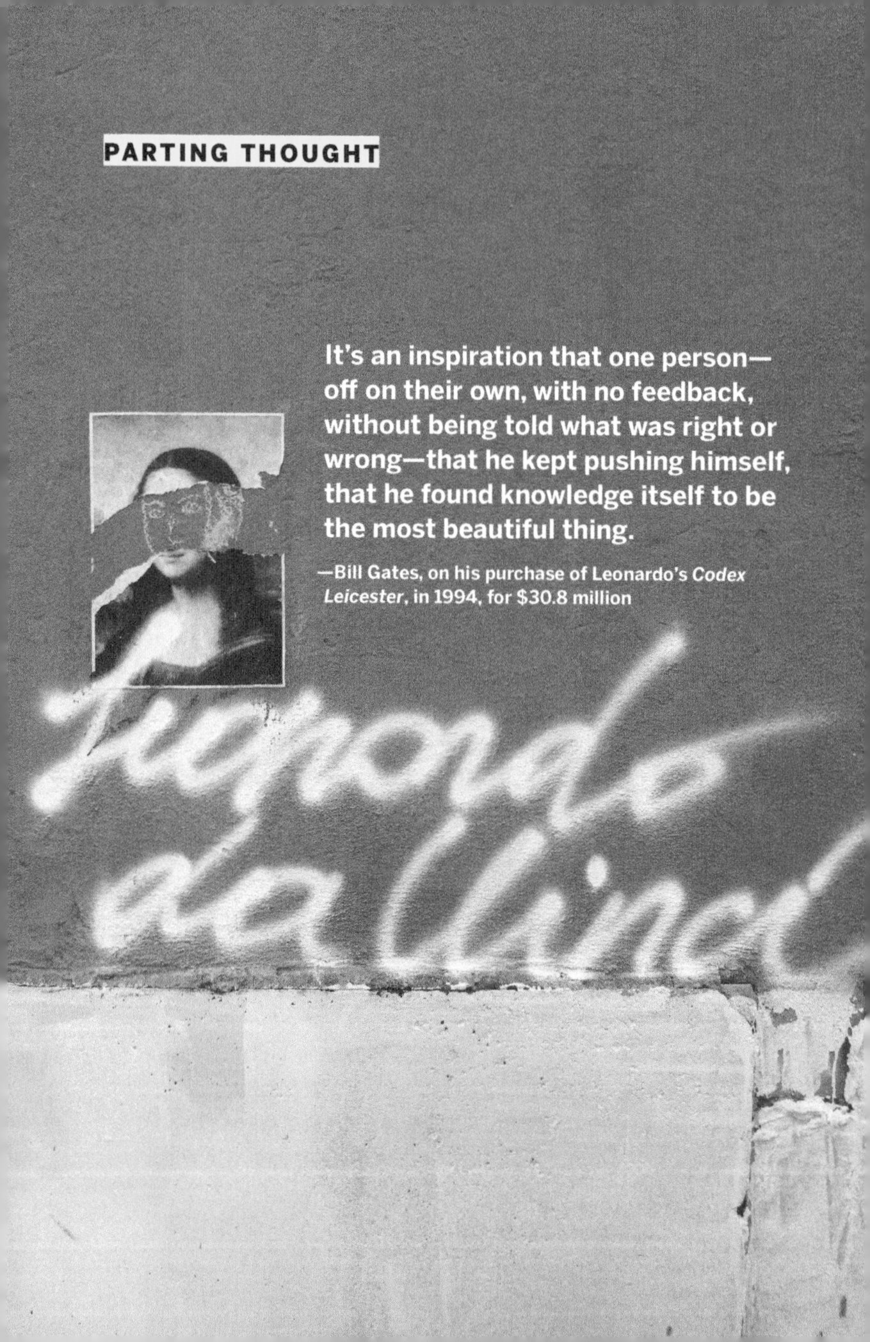

It's an inspiration that one person—off on their own, with no feedback, without being told what was right or wrong—that he kept pushing himself, that he found knowledge itself to be the most beautiful thing.

—Bill Gates, on his purchase of Leonardo's *Codex Leicester*, in 1994, for $30.8 million

SOURCES

Chauveau, Sophie. *Léonard da Vinci.* Paris: Flammarion, 2008.

Clayton, Martin, and Ronald Philo. *Leonardo da Vinci, Anatomist.* London: Royal Collection Publications, 2014.

Freud, Sigmund. *Eine Kindheitserinnerung des Leonardo da Vinci.* Leipzig: Deuticke, 1919.

Galluzzi, Paolo. *Gli ingegneri del Rinascimento. Da Brunelleschi a Leonardo da Vinci.* Florence: Giuli Editore, 1996.

——. La mente di Leonardo. *Nel laboratorio del genio universale.* Florence: Galleria degli Uffizi, 2006.

——. "Against Those 'Authors Who by Relying Only on Their Imagination Make Themselves Interpreters between Nature and Man,'" in Pietro C. Marani and Maria Teresa Fiorio, eds., *Leonardo da Vinci, 1452–1519: The Design of the World.* Milan: Skira, 2015. Pp. 261–269.

Kemp, Martin. *Leonardo da Vinci: The Marvellous Works of Nature and Man.* Oxford and New York: Oxford University Press, 2006.

"Leonardo da Vinci's *Codex on the Flight of Birds.*" Smithsonian National Air and Space Museum. Exhibit closed October 23, 2013. www.airandspace.si.edu/exhibitions/codex/

Leonardo da Vinci's Inventions. Accessed July 18, 2015. www.leonardodavincisinventions.com

Leonardo da Vinci. *Notebooks.* Ed. and trans. Irma A. Richter and Thereza Wells. Oxford and New York: Oxford University Press, 2008.

Marani, Pietro C., and Maria Teresa Fiorio, eds. *Leonardo da Vinci,* 1452-1519: *The Design of the World.* Milan: Skira, 2015.

Panofsky, Erwin. *The Codex Huygens and Leonardo da Vinci's Art Theory.* London: The Warburg Institute, 1940.

Rosenthal, Elizabeth. "In Italy, a Redesign of Nature to Clean It," New York Times. Accessed September 28, 2015. www.nytimes.com/2008/09/22/world/europe/22marsh.html?_r=1

Tucker, Rebecca, and Paul Crenshaw. *Discovering Leonardo: The Art Lover's Guide to Understanding Leonardo's Masterpieces.* New York: Universe, 2011.

Vasari, Giorgio. *Lives of the Most Eminent Painters, Sculptors, and Architects.* Vols. I-X, trans. Gaston du C. De Vere, London: Macmillan and the Medici Society, 1912–15 [1550].

Villata, Edoardo. *Leonardo da Vinci. I documenti e le testimonianze contemporanee.* Milan: Castello Sforzesco, 1999.

——. "Leonardo's Dreams: Natural Flight, Mechanical Flight, and Flights of the Imagination," in Pietro C. Marani and Maria Teresa Fiorio, eds., *Leonardo da Vinci, 1452–1519: The Design of the World.* Milan: Skira, 2015. Pp. 303–321.

CREDITS

For general information on our other products and services or to obtain technical support, please contact our Customer Care Department within the United States at (866) 744-2665, or outside the United States at (510) 253-0500.

Lightning Guides publishes its books in a variety of electronic and print formats. Some content that appears in print may not be available in electronic books, and vice versa.

ISBN Print 978-1-942411-90-1
eBook 978-1-942411-91-8

Front Cover: cl3m/www.cl3m.com
Backcover: © PRISMA ARCHIVO/Alamy Stock Photo
Interior Photos: © Dennis Hallinan/Alamy Stock Photo, p.1; © PRISMA ARCHIVO/Alamy Stock Photo, p.2; JUSTIN TALLIS/AFP/Getty Images, p.12; © Bettmann/Corbis, p.16; © Museo Ideale Leonardo Da Vinci, p.21; © Peter Horree/Alamy Stock Photo, p.23; Giorgio Magini/Stocksy, p.24; © Ilene MacDonald/Alamy Stock Photo. p.28; © RMN-Grand Palais/Art Resource, NY, p.32-33; © B Christopher/Alamy Stock Photo, p.35 © FineArt/Alamy Stock Photo, p.36; Alik Keplicz/AP Photo, p.39; © Heritage Image Partnership Ltd/Alamy Stock Photo, p.41; © liszt collection/Alamy Stock Photo, p.42; © Karl Kost/Alamy Stock Photo, p.44; © Heritage Image Partnership Ltd/Alamy Stock Photo, p.49; Bucchi Francesco/Shutterstock, p.52; © Masterpics/Alamy Stock Photo, p.52; Kiev.Victor/Shutterstock.com, p.52; Kiev.Victor/Shutterstock.com, p.52; © The Protected Art Archive/Alamy Stock Photo, p.52; © Karl Kost/Alamy Stock Photo, p.53; Georgios Kollidas/Shutterstock, p.53; © Everett Collection Inc/Alamy Stock Photo, p.53; Everett Historical/Shutterstock, p.53; trekandshoot/Shutterstock.com, p.53; © Keystone Pictures USA/Alamy Stock Photo, p.53; Beretta/Sims/Rex/REX USA, p.55; © FineArt/Alamy Stock Photo, p.56; © FineArt/Alamy Stock Photo, p.57; © John Baran/Alamy Stock Photo, p.58; © Dennis Hallinan/Alamy Stock Photo, p.58; © Karl Kost/Alamy Stock Photo, p.58; Nicole LaCoursiere, p.60-61; © Everett Collection Historical/Alamy, p.64; © Hemis/Alamy Stock Photo, p.69; © PAINTING/Alamy Stock Photo, p.73; Courtesy KNUT BRY, p.73; EPA/BAS CZERWINSKI, p.73; © Dennis Hallinan/Alamy Stock Photo, p.73; Igor I. Sikorsky Historical Archives, Inc, p.74; © Daily Mail/Rex/Alamy Stock Photo, p.79; Alinari/Art Resource, NY, p.83; © Gisuke Hagiwara/amanaimages/Corbis, p.82-83; © PRISMA ARCHIVO/Alamy Stock Photo, p.87; World History Archive/Alamy, p.90; © Dennis Hallinan / Alamy Stock Photo p.95; © GraphicaArtis/Corbis, p.96; © Alinari Archives/Corbis, p.102; © PAINTING/Alamy Stock Photo, p.105; © INTERFOTO/Alamy Stock Photo, p.110; © MARKA/Alamy Stock Photo, p.110; © Iberfoto/Everett Collection, p.111; © FineArt/Alamy Stock Photo, p.111; Georgios Kollidas/Shutterstock, p.112; © Gari Wyn Williams/Alamy Stock Photo, p.114

Lightning Source UK Ltd.
Milton Keynes UK
UKOW07f0616270416

273053UK00006B/17/P

9 781942 411901